Peacefully Parenting Adult Children

Minimize Struggles, Navigate Shifting Dynamics, and Build Strong and Resilient Relationships

Karen M. Carlson

Table of Contents

Trigger Warning

I lovingly dedicate this book to:
- ❖ My parents and in-laws who modeled parenting
- ❖ My husband who journeys this parenting path with me hand in hand
- ❖ My sons, their wives, and our grandchildren who grace us with love and forgiveness

---

"Embrace the journey to a happier, more peaceful family life with "Peacefully Parenting Adult Children."

"Peacefully Parenting Adult Children" is the must-read guide for transforming your relationship with your adult children. Packed with powerful insights and heartfelt advice, it's the ultimate tool for building stronger, more empathetic family connections. This book doesn't just suggest improvements; it delivers profound, life-changing strategies."

Jim Van Wyck

Introduction

Remember "no"? That two-letter word that dominated your toddler's vocabulary? Buckle up, parents, because you've graduated to an era of "why?"—a phase 2.0 interrogation masterpiece that elevates questioning to an art form. Suddenly, scraped knees and bedtime battles seem simple compared to the intricate labyrinth of parenting adult children.

You may have envisioned their graduation as a bittersweet victory lap, the culmination of years poured into bedtime stories, scraped knees, and endless cups of juice. Now, you stand staring at a new frontier—teeming with complexities that leave you feeling more lost than Dorothy in Oz. No champagne toast to mark this new stage? Fear not, seasoned veterans! Millions of you grapple with letting go while holding close. The negotiation between autonomy and support, the communication clashes over boundaries—it's enough to make even the calmest person crack.

But breathe; you're not alone in this emotional jungle. I stand in your shoes. As the parent of three adult sons, I've known the joys, frustrations, and roller coaster ride of emotions navigating this terrain. I have been able to enjoy watching them take their first wobbly steps as toddlers, seeing them try to figure themselves out in adolescence, and becoming self-sustaining adults. My journey has yielded firsthand insights and strategies, both triumphs and stumbles, that I share in this book. My children have taught me many things about parenting, and life in general. We'll learn how to navigate the complexities of parenting adult children—sons and daughters alike—while staying sane and thriving in our own lives. "Peacefully Parenting Adult Children" is your refuge. This is your survival guide, your compass, pointing the way through twists and turns with grace, humor, and empathy.

This isn't an academic book. It's a toolbox full of practical strategies, real-life stories, and insights gleaned from experience. We'll explore the evolving dynamics of the adult-child relationship, master "grown-up" communication, and learn to set boundaries without being overly restrictive.

This journey isn't just about letting go. You'll tackle setting boundaries that empower your adult child without turning into Attila the Hun and navigate conflicts when their "why?" turns into a full-blown hurricane—financial woes, dating disasters, existential crises—you name it, we've got you covered.

When you finish this book, you will be ready to respond to life's unexpected challenges. At the end of this book you will be equipped to support your adult child through addiction, self-discovery, relationships, and so much more. Together, we'll redefine family roles as grandchildren enter the picture, in-laws become permanent fixtures, and your retirement dreams morph into road trip detours.

The chasms that can open between parent and adult child are often more impressive than the Grand Canyon. We will address communication issues, repair damaged relationships, and rediscover the joys of connection, even when the path seems difficult to navigate.

We won't forget about you because a burnt-out parent can't help anyone, especially themselves. Self-care isn't selfish; it's the essential support you need to navigate this journey effectively.

We'll explore how to maintain your well-being while supporting your adult child, finding a balance between giving them space and being present. Along the way, we'll address common parenting pitfalls and the importance of letting go of control. With practical exercises and actionable advice, you'll be equipped to navigate this rewarding and challenging phase of parenting with confidence and grace. Together, we'll embark on a journey of self-discovery, resilience, and profound connection with our adult children. Let's get started!

"Peacefully Parenting Adult Children" is more than just a book; it's a promise. A promise of hope, understanding, and building stronger, more fulfilling relationships with your adult offspring, no matter how challenging the path ahead. So, grab your metaphorical hiking boots, put on your bravest smile, and let's embark on this adventure together. Remember, you're not lost; you're simply charting a new course. And with the right tools and a dash of humor, this journey can be more rewarding than you ever imagined.

When you finish reading this book, I promise ~
- You will no longer feel like an island, stranded and lost
- You will understand many strategies to make significant changes that benefit both you and your adult sons and/or daughters
- You will see possibilities you never expected

In the following chapters, we'll dive deeper into the intricacies of navigating this uncharted territory of parenting adult children. We'll explore how to communicate effectively, establish healthy boundaries, and support your adult child through life's ups and downs. Whether you're dealing with financial challenges, relationship struggles, or existential crises, we've got you covered. Together, we'll equip you with the tools and strategies you need to navigate this phase with confidence and grace. So, let's prepare and continue this journey of peaceful parenting together. Ready to ditch chaos for peace?

From "Weaver of Words" by Karen M. Carlson

You Taught Me

As I look back and think back

on my days of being your mother,

I realize you taught me how to be a mother

before you even arrived.

The lessons you taught,

and yet still are teaching

change still, change always.

The love came forth in exhaustion and joy.

Love to hold, love to hug, love to borrow,

if only for a while.

This love is a strong link,

ever present, ever treasured.

Though miles may be many,

you teach me, and I learn,

what it means to be Mother.

"Peacefully Parenting Adult Children" is written as a guidebook to treacherous territory. How do you trust the relationship you've built with your children to withstand independence, empty nests and your own urge to "help" as you did when they were little? This book gives you simple, practical steps to grow into the next phase of your life as a treasured friend and consultant. Love it!

Denise S.

"This information is so important for parents to get before all the challenges start punching them in the gut."

Kim B.

"I could really relate to the section about shifting my relationship from being the authoritarian parent to the supportive parent using our common background. Listening, offering suggestions, taking their spouse into consideration are all important suggestions."

Brigitte D.

"Treating our children like adults often challenges us to grow up too! Karen Carlson shows us how both parent and child benefit when we learn how to "let go" while still holding them close.

Dr. Jim Healy
President, Rooted in Love

Part 1: Minimize Struggles

Remember the emotions as you held your precious newborn for the first time? The endless nights, the love, the pride as they took their first steps and said "mama" or "dada"? Every milestone and challenge shaped your bond, building an unbreakable connection. Now, the landscape shifts. Your adult children aren't babes anymore but young adults venturing into adulthood. This transition, filled with joy and pride, can trigger a mix of emotions in parents – excitement, fear, uncertainty, and even a tinge of loss. Gone are the days of constant presence, unwavering dependence, and comforting routines. Instead, a new landscape emerges, leaving you with questions as your adult child embarks on adulthood. How do you navigate this shift in your relationship, ensuring their freedom without severing the cord? How do you bridge the generation gap, fostering effective communication that balances respect for their newfound independence with your support and guidance? And how do you establish healthy boundaries that nurture trust and mutual understanding, paving the way for a thriving relationship? Part 1 will equip you with tools and strategies to face them.

Minimize Struggles is your roadmap to navigating this transformative phase with confidence and connection. Brace yourself for the emotional ups and downs as your child transitions into adulthood! We'll equip you with practical tools to navigate this exciting yet sometimes challenging journey. We'll delve deep into the developmental changes shaping your adult child and their impact on your relationship, helping you understand their evolving needs and perspectives. We'll guide you through mastering the art of communication, equipping you to navigate difficult conversations, express your needs respectfully, and actively listen for stronger bonds. Setting healthy boundaries is crucial, and we'll provide strategies to empower your adult child's independence while maintaining a supportive presence in their lives. Financial complexities won't faze you either, as we'll tackle issues like financial assistance, setting boundaries, and planning for the future together. And let's not forget about the Empty Nest Syndrome. We'll explore self-discovery, help you build new routines, and ensure you maintain fulfilling relationships beyond your role as a parent. So, take a deep breath, embrace the change, and get ready to thrive alongside your adult child – Part 1 has your back!

This journey is not about clinging to the past but embracing a new chapter filled with unique joys and challenges. With the appropriate tools and a positive mindset, you can cultivate a flourishing relationship with your adult child based on mutual respect, love, and understanding.

Chapter 1: From Full Hearts to Unfurled Wings—Launching Your Adult Children With Grace

The silence descends subtly, at first an unfamiliar quietude settling into the corners of your home. The echoes of laughter and hurried footsteps fade, replaced by a stillness that both soothes and stings. Your children, once nestled within the vibrant melody of your family life, have spread their wings and embarked on their own journeys. This is the bittersweet beauty of the empty nest—a profound shift that carries its own symphony of emotions.

Embracing the Empty Nest

This new chapter comes with an undeniable sense of loss. The silence rings where echoes of laughter used to bounce, and routines you held dear have flown the coop with your fledgling adults. Grief is natural, a testament to your love for raising them. Soothe those emotions, talk it out, and seek support—you're not alone in this. Countless parents have harmonized with this melody, and communities like "Empty Nest Parents" offer understanding chords of comfort. As the old saying goes, distance can be a blessing or a curse. While I sometimes miss the daily moments with my adult children, the space also allows me to focus on my personal growth and rediscover passions I set aside during my busy parenting years. It's a delicate balance, but I'm learning to appreciate both the closeness and the distance, cherishing the unique connections we maintain. Before your adult child leaves home, have open conversations about potential challenges they might face, like time management, social pressures, and academic responsibility. This can help them feel prepared and supported.

But amidst the loss, a new melody hums—a chance to acknowledge and navigate the emotions that arise during this transition, an opportunity to rediscover yourself. Empty Nest Syndrome is a real phenomenon characterized by feelings of loneliness, sadness, and even grief. It's normal to miss your children and the routines you shared. Honor these feelings, allow yourself to process them, and know that you're not alone. Remember the person you were before the joyful chaos of parenthood filled your days? Dust off those passions, hobbies, and dreams that are tucked away. Pick up your guitar, join that painting class, and write that novel—it's your encore!

But wait, isn't that "facing emotions" stuff missing? Don't worry—it's woven in! Grieving is a journey, not a destination. Mourn the routines, companionship, and primary caregiver role, but honor them and move through gently. This isn't the end of your parenting song; it's just a beautiful modulation in your journey. Be kind to yourself, and rewrite your definition of fulfillment in this new act.

Now, take a breath. The empty nest might seem jarring at first, but it's not a solo performance. Dive into books, articles, and podcasts; connect with others navigating similar waters. Sharing these experiences is an anchor, reminding you you're not alone.

Here's the twist: reframe the empty nest! Instead of an end, see it as a new beginning. Imagine personal growth, self-discovery, and a deeper connection with your adult children. Let go of societal expectations and write your own fulfilling verse in this new act.

The melody changes. Once filled with children's laughter, it now holds space for your inner music. You're always young enough to learn! This is the perfect time to take online classes, join a community college program, or pursue a lifelong dream. Rediscover it! Dust off that guitar, explore painting, and write that book. Reconnect with forgotten hobbies, discover new passions, and let hidden harmonies blossom. Take time to celebrate your strengths and accomplishments. Write a list of things you're good at and what makes you proud. This can boost your confidence and help you move forward with excitement.

You're not just rediscovering passions; you're rediscovering yourself. Who were you before parenthood took center stage? What brings you joy, challenges you, and makes you feel truly alive? Explore activities that nourish your soul and discover new facets of yourself. Self-care isn't a luxury; it's essential. Prioritize your well-being, meditate, exercise, and connect with loved ones. A healthy and happy you are the perfect score for facing this transition and building a fulfilling life beyond the empty nest. Everyone experiences this transition differently. Comparing yourself to others won't help. Embrace your own unique emotions and journey.

Shifting Focus: From Parenting to Pursuing Personal Passions

Think of this as your "second act," a time to explore, learn, and grow. The empty nest isn't an ending but a thrilling second act: a time for self-discovery, personal growth, and strengthening your connection with your adult children. Embrace lifelong learning through online platforms like MasterClass. Pursue forgotten hobbies or ignite new passions, join clubs, and connect with like-minded individuals. Support your community through volunteering and discovering fulfillment in assisting others. The world is full of opportunities!

My husband and I recently joined a Chamber of Commerce, offering us a great way to connect with new people and engage in thought-provoking discussions. This social interaction fulfills a need I didn't realize I had and complements my personal wellness business. It's important to remember that our needs and interests change throughout life, and the empty nest can be a chance to explore new sources of fulfillment beyond our customary roles (Caine, n.d.).

Rediscover aspects of the person you were. What did you dream of? What brought you joy? Dust off those interests, explore your talents, and reconnect with your true self. Don't limit yourself! Step out of your comfort zone and try something different: painting, coding, or writing. Caine believes self-care is essential. Feed your soul with activities that provide peace and joy, like meditation, exercise, nature, or old friends.

As you begin this second act, your relationship with your adult children continues. They may be physically distant, but your emotional connection remains. Shift from "parent" to "consultant," offering guidance and support when asked but respecting their independence and choices. Celebrate their victories and be their sounding board. Embrace different ways to stay connected: plan video calls, schedule visits, and share experiences through online games or hobbies. Encourage their growth, share your experiences, and cultivate mutual respect and understanding.

Your second act is about creating a new, fulfilling family dynamic. Reclaim your identity, pursue your passions, and nurture your connection with your adult children. This new chapter can be a beautiful symphony of self-discovery and shared joy, enriching your lives.

Transitioning From Parent to Consultant

We never really release our children completely, and don't want to. An important shift for me was not calling them my 'kids' anymore. It can become so unconscious to refer to them that way, but they are not kids, they are adults. I had to intentionally change my vocabulary to saying 'my son' or simply call them by their name. It might seem like a minor thing but acknowledging that they are not my children anymore but my sons made a big difference. Coping with a sense of release can be challenging, but as they enter adulthood, your role shifts from parent to consultant. This empowers them to make their own choices, learn from their experiences, and thrive.

Respect their individuality. They're unique, with their own perspectives and journeys. Offer guidance, sharing your wisdom with phrases like "From my experience..." or "Have you considered...". Skip ultimatums: their voice and perspective deserve to be heard and valued, even when they disagree. Disagreements are inevitable but navigate them respectfully. Engage in open communication, actively listening without judgment.

Open communication bridges this transition. Actively listen to their hopes, anxieties, and dreams. Validate their feelings, establishing a safe space for honest conversation. Embrace the evolving relationship, cherishing the unique melody it creates.

Trust is the foundation. Empower them by trusting their judgment and capabilities. Becoming a consultant fosters independence and mature decision-making. This means giving them space for their choices, even if they differ from yours. Be their supportive safety net, not a rule-setter or decision-maker. Mistakes are valuable learning opportunities; let them navigate, offering support when needed.

Communication is a two-way street. Actively listen without interrupting or dismissing their feelings. Validate their emotions, even if you disagree. Focus on understanding their perspective, fostering trust, and strengthening your bond.

This empty nest isn't an ending but a vibrant new chapter. Embrace the space to explore passions, rediscover hobbies, and embark on new adventures. Encourage their growth, celebrating their achievements. This is an exciting opportunity for personal development. As you evolve together, your relationship deepens and enriches, creating a beautiful harmony in your lives.

Keeping the Lines Open: Essential Communication Strategies for Empty Nesters

As you close this chapter and step into the vast possibilities of your second act, remember that the silence in your home doesn't signal the end of your connection with your adult children. It's a shift in its melody. The laughter may no longer echo, but the love and shared experiences remain, waiting to be woven into a new, richer harmony.

Open communication is the invisible thread that binds your relationships. Don't underestimate the power of a simple "How are you feeling?" or "Tell me about your day." These gestures show you care, even when you are physically distant. Profound conversations often start with straightforward questions, opening doors to deeper understanding and strengthening the invisible bond.

This journey of change may have moments of awkward silence and uncertain notes, but communication is your guiding light. Let it keep you connected, not just as parent and adult child but as individuals on intertwined paths. Embrace the new rhythm, cherish the evolving melody, and remember that beautiful symphonies often start with a single, heartfelt note.

As you close this first chapter on embracing the empty nest and turning your focus to yourself, take a moment to reflect on your journey.

- What hobbies or interests did you put aside when raising children? What excites you now? List the possibilities you'd like to explore further.
- How do you define yourself beyond being a parent? What qualities and experiences shape your unique identity? List five words describing who you are at this stage.
- What long-term goals did you put on hold? Imagine your desired future and jot down key steps to move towards it.

- Reflect on your strengths and experiences, beyond parenting. List the skills or talents you can offer.
- Who could benefit from your expertise or experience? Families facing similar transitions? Specific groups within your community?
- How can you communicate healthy boundaries with your adult children while maintaining close connections? Reflect on an area where setting more explicit boundaries might be beneficial.
- Do you hold back your opinions or desires to avoid conflict? How can you communicate your needs and feelings more authentically while respecting others?
- Do you genuinely listen to your adult child's experiences or offer unsolicited advice? Reflect on a recent conversation and identify opportunities to practice active listening more effectively.

Are you ready to rewrite your connection? Turn the page and let's begin a new chapter, where communication unlocks a deeper relationship with your adult children, even as your empty nest echoes with memories of laughter and love.

Chapter 2: Communication Styles— the Power of Words

As seasons change and families evolve, so do the dynamics of our relationships. Whether you're navigating the uncharted waters of your adult child's independence, cherishing the unique bond with your teenage grandchild, or simply fostering connections across a generational divide, one element remains ever-present: communication. It is the cornerstone of understanding, the bridge across divides, and the language of love that transcends age.

This chapter explores the transformative power of communication in these precious connections. We'll explore the diverse range of communication styles, unveil strategies for navigating even the trickiest situations, and unlock the magic of active listening. Ultimately, we'll discover that mastering this essential skill is more than just speaking and being heard; it's about truly seeing, appreciating, and connecting with loved ones on our ever-evolving journey.

Active Listening: Tuning In to Truly Connect

As your child becomes an adult, your relationship evolves. Whether you're facing an empty nest, bonding with a grandchild, or navigating the subtleties of "grown and flown" connections, communication is key. But in this "second act," effective communication goes beyond words. It requires fluency in the language of love and understanding, where active listening is crucial.

Active listening isn't passive silence. It's an immersive journey requiring your full attention as you delve into your adult child's perspective. Imagine yourself as a detective, gathering clues from their words, body language, and unspoken emotions. This unlocks a deeper understanding, fosters empathy, and strengthens the emotional bond.

Why is active engagement crucial? Studies show active listening significantly strengthens parent-child relationships, even as children enter adulthood (Birditt et al., 2009). It's an antidote to frustration, diffuses conflict, and builds an emotional bridge across the "generation gap."

Ready to become a master of active listening? Here's what you could do:

- Reflect on their thoughts with nuance to ensure understanding. "It sounds like you're feeling..." opens the door to a deeper connection.
- Go beyond "yes" or "no" answers. Invite them to elaborate with inquiries like, "Tell me more about what led you to feel this way." This fosters trust and connection.
- Acknowledge their feelings with empathy, not judgment. A simple "It sounds like you're frustrated. I can see why you're feeling that way" speaks volumes.
- Show understanding without taking sides. Phrases like, "That must be challenging. I can see why you're overwhelmed." demonstrate compassion and build bridges.

Active listening is a lifelong performance, not a one-act show. It demands patience, practice, and adaptation. Consider individual preferences and cultural variations. Technology, a double-edged sword, needs thoughtful handling. Use its potential for connection, but avoid distractions.

By mastering active listening, you'll create a deeper connection with your adult child, transforming your relationship's "second act" into a masterpiece of love, understanding, and shared wisdom.

Bridging the Communication Gap: Focused Styles

Every generation brings unique perspectives and preferences to life. It surely keeps life interesting, doesn't it? As your relationship with your adult child evolves, bridging the communication gap is crucial for strengthening those connections. "Miscommunication or misunderstanding is the number one reason why so many tough conversations escalate to uncomfortable levels of tension, resentment, or lack of trust. How can we share our feelings and perspectives with our children and be heard without causing hurt, anger, or silence? How can we have a close relationship with our children if we avoid meaningful conversation? The answers to these questions pose some of our biggest challenges as parents" (Davis, 2017). Effective communication isn't about imposing your style but embracing its richness.

Stepping Into Their World

Ditch the "my way or the highway" mentality. Explore their preferred platforms: texting, video calls, and social media. It shows respect for their communication style. Technology can be a bridge, not a barrier. Peek into their social media world to gain insights, but respect their privacy. Unsolicited advice (momsplaining) backfires quickly. Seek common ground: mix phone calls with emojis or video chats with letters. Communication is a two-way street paved with flexibility and understanding.

When adult children are launched, they may have a significant other who may be a spouse, which becomes important to understand. This person has their own background and financial history, likely influencing your son or daughter more than their own history. When my sons got serious with someone, it was time to observe quietly from a distance. My opinions would most likely not be well received and would be translated as criticism more often than not. Building a stable and caring relationship with the person my son chose was important. Waiting until they asked a question or opened the door to some part of my life experience was important. What one in-law may be open to hearing was different than another. Being respectful and not overbearing was important for building each relationship uniquely for the short-term and long-term as well.

Beyond Generational Labels

It's true, generational labels offer a starting point for understanding communication preferences. Different generations tend to favor specific methods and styles. Baby Boomers often gravitate toward face-to-face interactions, Millennials towards digital messaging, and so on. However, remembering that everyone is shaped by unique experiences and cultural influences is crucial. A "boomerang child" returning home to live with parents after living independently, might prefer open, collaborative communication. A "sandwich generation" individual who cares for both aging parents and their own children might appreciate concise and direct messages due to time constraints. So, while generational preferences provide a framework, embracing the individual and their unique story fosters effective communication.

The Art of Active Listening

Communication transcends speaking; it's genuinely listening. Actively engage with their perspective, even when it differs. Empathize with their feelings and avoid judgment. Ask open-ended questions that invite elaboration and foster understanding. Mirror their words and paraphrase key points for clarity. Active listening strengthens emotional connections, building trust and stronger relationships.

Acknowledging Differences, Embracing Connections

The "generation gap" exists for a reason. Different age groups have distinct preferences. Be understanding and adapt your communication style. Gen Z might prioritize quick responses and visual communication, while Gen X might prefer concise emails. Recognizing these differences shows respect and opens doors to meaningful connections.

Technology: A Bridge, Not a Replacement

Geography may separate you, but technology offers tools to stay connected. Remember that funny family photo? Share it on Facebook or Instagram to spark laughter and memories across the miles. Longing for a face-to-face chat? Schedule a video call on Zoom or FaceTime—a lifeline for older generations. Collaborate on projects using platforms like Google Docs for teamwork. Use digital storytelling to create shared photo albums or video presentations. Embrace technology as a bridge, not a barrier, to stay connected. Use it creatively, but maintain authenticity and personal connection.

Respecting Boundaries

Effective communication isn't just about words; it's about building understanding and respect. This journey requires sensitivity to individual boundaries, regardless of age. While some generations thrive on directness, others may appreciate a gentler approach. Avoid overly critical or intrusive communication. Genuine support lies in offering a listening ear rather than unsolicited advice. Be present and watch for disengagement signals. Respecting their need for space or privacy fosters trust. Establish clear boundaries. Discuss preferred communication methods and response times. Respecting these subtleties unlocks deeper connections.

Building Bridges, One Conversation at a Time

Open dialogue and mutual understanding are crucial to building lasting relationships. It starts with truly hearing the other person by acknowledging their perspective. Find common ground to anchor the discussion, and phrase your arguments in a positive, solution-oriented way. Ditch justifications and explanations; focus on open-ended questions and active listening. Communication is a journey, not a destination. Embrace the adventure of connecting.

Tailoring Your Approach

While these core principles provide a strong foundation, communication goes beyond one-size-fits-all. Weave in generation-specific strategies to connect. Humor resonates with Millennials, while Gen X might appreciate clear agendas. Your secret weapon is emotional intelligence! This superpower allows you to understand and manage your own emotions, recognize, and respond to others' emotions, and tune into your adult child's emotional landscape, fostering understanding and bridging the generational divide. Be patient, practice these principles consistently, and adapt your approach as needed. With dedication and flexibility, you'll speak the same language, even if the dialect differs slightly.

Navigating Difficult Conversations

Life is full of challenges and obstacles that can test our relationships and communication with our adult children. Just as a river encounters rapids on its journey, our interactions with our adult children can involve difficult moments that require careful navigation and understanding. Given the ever-evolving dynamic and inherent power dynamics, navigating these stretches between parent and adult child can feel daunting. But fear not! Mindfulness, empathy, and essential tools become your allies in transforming challenges into opportunities.

Imagine setting sail into churning rapids without proper preparation. It wouldn't be wise, would it? The same applies to difficult conversations. Before engaging, ensure your vessel is seaworthy. Ditch the accusatory "you" and use "I'" statements instead. Owning your feelings with "I feel hurt when..." fosters understanding better than finger-pointing. You're not the captain of the other person's emotions but of your own. Acknowledge your biases and keep them from steering the conversation off course. Take a deep breath and employ calming techniques if needed; the goal is a collaborative journey, not a one-sided victory.

Guilt trips don't work anymore! I've learned firsthand that trying to make my adult son feel guilty about something is ineffective. It's often as subtle as a brick. What might have worked when he was younger doesn't resonate anymore. He told me straight-up, "Mom, guilt trips don't work anymore." That honest feedback was a turning point. It was time I reframed how I communicated, acknowledging that they had the freedom to respond as they saw fit. Power imbalances can creep in and have a negative impact, but that doesn't mean we can't maintain respect and equality even during disagreements. It's crucial to shift from manipulation to understanding, using "I" statements to express feelings without blame. Actively listening with empathy, trying to see their perspective, fosters a genuine connection and allows us to navigate challenging conversations constructively. A strong foundation of mutual respect and trust is vital to building open communication, minimizing the need for guilt trips. I believe the key is learning how to have an adult conversation, including disagreement, and emerge without injury.

Now that you're ready, it's time to set sail. Choose a calm moment, free from emotional downpours or exhaustion. Communication is a two-way street, not a monologue. Give your full attention, validate their feelings, and truly listen. Listen actively by asking clarifying questions and paraphrasing their points to ensure understanding. This builds empathy, allowing you to navigate the rapids together.

Instead of blaming and complaining, imagine yourselves as a team weathering the storm. Shift your focus from fault to collaborative problem-solving. Brainstorm solutions that meet everyone's needs; be open to learning from each other and charting new courses. Growth happens everywhere, even in unexpected conversations. Be open to collaboration, for solutions often lie in surprising places.

Consider the other person's communication style. Some might respond better to directness, while others prefer a more indirect approach. Identify shared values and goals amidst differences. This creates unity and purpose, reminding you that you're both on the same boat, navigating the same challenges.

Difficult conversations may not resolve all issues instantly. Set realistic expectations to foster understanding and progress. Even the mightiest rivers have calm stretches. If emotions escalate or fatigue sets in, take breaks to cool down and regain composure. Return to the conversation when you are ready for a more productive dialogue. Patience and understanding are essential.

Consider seeking guidance from a therapist, mediator, or trusted friend for challenging situations. Their insights can help navigate complex situations. Celebrate the small wins and progress made during the conversation. Acknowledge each other's efforts and reinforce positive communication patterns for future open dialogue. Every step forward is a victory in navigating life's challenges together.

Difficult conversations should not be feared but embraced as opportunities for connection and growth. Approach them with empathy, a willingness to compromise, and a focus on finding solutions together. With these tools and a spirit of collaboration, you can navigate life's challenges with confidence and grace, emerging stronger and closer than before.

Navigating the parent adult-child relationship requires being attentive and adaptable. In this dynamic, be mindful of the power imbalance and respect their autonomy. Maintaining open communication is essential. Finding a balance between care and control and creating an environment that encourages open dialogue is important. This journey is a marathon, not a sprint. Expect bumps, misunderstandings, and growth. Embrace the calm in the middle of chaos. Together, navigate with patience, persistence, and a willingness to adjust.

Difficult conversations can be challenging, but they unite. Face them together and watch your bond with your adult child deepen. Embark with an open mind, curiosity, and a willingness to navigate any challenges. With these tools, you can navigate life's ups and downs with confidence, and if the outcome isn't what you might have hoped for, you have given it your best effort. You can always try again. Don't give up.

Curbing the Urge to Momsplain (and Dadsplain)

The path to adulthood isn't just a one-way street of unsolicited advice. Our good intentions can lead to "momsplaining" or "dadsplaining"—offering solutions or opinions when they're not wanted—which can backfire. It can erode trust, create distance, and make adult children feel like their autonomy is under attack.

How can we build a respectful and meaningful relationship with our adult child?

The Art of Letting Go: Embracing Their Sovereignty

From planning their every step to cheering them on from the sidelines, your role as a parent transforms alongside your adult child's journey. This shift presents a beautiful opportunity for a deeper connection. Imagine yourself as a supportive coach guiding them with a "lighthouse beam" of encouragement, not forceful control.

Create a safe space for genuine dialogue without judgment. Understand their point of view by listening and asking questions before advising. Genuine connection thrives on empathy, which involves gathering information and building bridges.

Celebrate their individuality! Encourage them to explore their passions and revel in their unique talents and perspectives. Recognize and appreciate their growth, reminding them of your pride. Embrace lifelong learning, acknowledging they have knowledge and experiences you don't have. See yourselves as co-travelers on a journey of mutual discovery, enriching each other's perspective.

By embracing the shift from conductor to coach, you cultivate a connection built on mutual respect, trust, and the joy of watching them soar.

Beyond Universals: Acknowledging Variety in Connection

Communication isn't one-size-fits-all. Cultural background affects whether something feels intrusive or not. Genuine connection requires understanding the heart's language, not just spoken words. Both mothers and fathers can give too much advice, with different impacts based on their adult child's gender identity. Empathy means walking in their shoes, not just offering your perspective.

Healthy boundaries are essential. Talk openly with your adult child about helpful support and unwanted advice, creating a communication framework that respects closeness and individual space. Healthy boundaries are like fences, not walls; they allow for connection while respecting needs. Tailoring your communication to your adult child's unique personality and preferences lays the foundation for a thriving connection built on respect, empathy, and understanding.

A strong parent adult-child relationship is built on mutual respect, trust, and understanding. By letting go of unsolicited advice and embracing genuine communication, you can cultivate a deeper connection that thrives on shared love and support. Remember, this journey is an ongoing adventure. There will be misunderstandings, bumps, and missteps.

As you navigate this evolving relationship, unexpected detours are normal. Seek professional guidance when needed. Therapists and counselors specializing in family dynamics can offer fresh perspectives, communication tools, and empowerment. Extend forgiveness to yourself for unsolicited advice, and offer it to your adult child if their reaction stings. Learn from these experiences and move forward together. Celebrate every step, no matter how small. Milestones, shared laughter, and genuine connection are precious threads in your bond. Acknowledge these moments and let them fuel your growth as partners.

The most valuable gift for your adult child is your genuine presence, unwavering support, and belief in their abilities. Letting go of control and embracing a partnership built on respect and understanding can cultivate a thriving connection in this new chapter of your relationship.

Keeping the Lines Open: Mastering Difficult Conversations

As we close this chapter on communication, it's not a finite skill. It's a lifelong symphony played on the ever-changing instruments in our relationships. Embrace each connection's unique melodies, from playful friends to family dynamics. Practice active listening to guide understanding. Navigate challenges with empathy, allowing improvisation and shared interpretation. Revel in unexpected harmonies, moments of laughter, and shared tears. Communication isn't just about clarity; it's the emotional resonance that lingers. Take a moment to reflect.

- Reflect on a recent conversation with your adult child. Did you actively listen to their perspective? Were you mindful of your biases and emotional state? How could you have communicated more effectively?
- Consider your preferred communication style. Do you lean towards "momsplaining" or "dadsplaining"? How can you offer support and guidance without overstepping?
- What personal communication goals do you want to set for yourself? Do you want to become more patient in

difficult conversations, more open to different perspectives, or more comfortable expressing your emotions effectively?

- Choose a strategy from this chapter to practice next week. Identify a specific situation and implement it. How will you measure success?
- Think of someone in your life with a different communication style. How can you bridge the gap and improve understanding?
- Imagine a tough upcoming conversation. What steps can you take to prepare and navigate it productively?
- Write down a recent communication experience that left you frustrated or misunderstood. Reflect on the contributing factors, including your communication style and the other person's. What lessons can you learn from this?
- Imagine your ideal communication style. What qualities does it embody? How can you start incorporating them into your everyday interactions?

By fostering genuine connections, you weave a tapestry of relationships that enrich your life—a vibrant artwork in progress.

Chapter 3: Charting New Routes— Finding Joy and Purpose in Later-Life Transitions

Life rarely follows a script, and even after your children have flown the nest, an unexpected detour might lead you to "silver splitting" or "grey divorce" later in life. While this presents an opportunity for rediscovery, freedom, and rewriting your narrative, navigating this transition, especially with separation, can be intimidating. Emotions run high, familiar landmarks disappear, and the future seems nebulous, like sailing a stormy sea.

This chapter is your compass through these choppy waters. We'll explore the social, emotional, and cultural shifts driving this trend, acknowledge the impact on your adult children, and equip you with tools for a new course filled with joy, purpose, and enduring connections. The journey may be challenging, but it's an opportunity for growth. So, adjust your sails, steady your resolve, and prepare for a fulfilling new chapter—a chance to shed outdated narratives, rewrite limiting beliefs, and embrace new possibilities.

"Silver splitting" isn't just a reaction to changing societal norms. Our understanding of love, companionship, and personal growth evolves. This chapter will explore unmet needs, changing priorities, communication challenges in relationships contributing to such decisions, and acknowledging complex internal landscapes. We'll also address the pressures of the "sandwich generation" caring for aging parents and adult children.

Divorce affects everyone, including adult children. We'll address their challenges, offering guidance on open communication, healthy boundaries, and supportive relationships with them, their partners, and your former spouse. The family dynamic may shift, but it doesn't have to define your future connections.

Equipped with this understanding, we'll empower you to navigate the practical and emotional aspects of this transition. From handling financial and legal intricacies to prioritizing your well-being through self-care, this chapter will provide actionable steps to guide you.

This journey isn't just about overcoming challenges; it's about rediscovering yourself and creating a fulfilling life. This chapter will inspire you to reconnect with forgotten passions, explore new interests, and embrace personal growth. Expanding your social circle and engaging in fulfilling activities will bring newfound support and companionship. Boldly embrace the unknown, ignite your journey with new experiences, and discover limitless possibilities.

Join me as we navigate this journey together. Understanding the landscape, navigating challenges, and embracing growth transform this transition, a chance to rewrite, redefine, and create a joyful, purposeful future.

Navigating the Sea of Change: Silver Splitting's Impact

Images of heartbroken children often come to mind when we think of divorce, but separation rates are rising among older parents with adult children. This is fueled by complex family changes. Understanding these dynamics can guide you through this transition.

The departure of children isn't just about "empty nest syndrome" or "boomerang kids." As family roles shift, individual needs and desires can too. Leaving can spark introspection, longing for personal growth, and re-evaluating fulfillment. Dreams put on hold for years may beckon, urging you to chase them with newfound freedom.

Long-held marriage expectations can lose their luster over time. The empty nest can become a canvas for pursuing unfulfilled dreams and seeking personal satisfaction. It's a chance to rewrite your life script, reclaiming passions and aspirations that may have dimmed.

Communication issues that have simmered for years can come to a boil when the constant chatter of children fades. This newfound quiet isn't just about hearing the refrigerator hum; it's about hearing each other clearly, perhaps for the first time in years. Though painful, this clarity can lead to a deeper understanding of incompatibility or a renewed commitment to communication and growth.

Acknowledging shifting priorities, unmet expectations, and communication challenges gives you insight into "silver splitting." While overwhelming, this transition can be an opportunity for personal growth and self-discovery. Embark on this journey with open eyes, a curious mind, and the knowledge that a fulfilling new chapter may await you at this stage of life.

Supporting Your Adult Children

Ending a marriage has far-reaching effects, especially on children. Even grown-up children are deeply affected by their parents' divorce, particularly later in life. Acknowledging and addressing their emotions and needs is essential. Although you're navigating your emotional hurricane, keeping their well-being at the helm is crucial. According to the Canadian Pediatric Society (2018), Kemp et al. (2023) and Noeder (2023), here's how to weather the storm together:

Prioritize transparency and open communication. Share decisions and feelings openly. They're adults, not children who need every detail of your experiences. Focus on the impact on their lives, acknowledging the challenges they'll face.

This is a significant change for them, so expect waves of emotions. Respect their feelings. Acknowledge their anger, sadness, or confusion without judgment. Offer a safe space for them to express themselves. They're not responsible for fixing your situation; they're just trying to understand it.

Resist involving them in the conflict or using them as emotional sounding boards against your ex. This puts them in a loyalty bind and strains your relationships. Let them know you're available to listen, but they're not your therapist or confidante in this conflict.

While supporting, establishing, and maintaining healthy boundaries, don't rely on them for emotional fulfillment. Build your own support system through friends, family, or therapy. Even the most generous well runs dry. By caring for yourself, you'll be better equipped to be there.

By practicing open communication, respecting their emotions, avoiding triangulation, and maintaining healthy boundaries, you can help your adult children navigate divorce. You're not alone; together, you can find calmer seas.

Exploring New Horizons Together

"Silver splitting" presents unique challenges compared to traditional divorces. Once your children have left, their absence can create a void, leaving you questioning your future relationships and identity. Finances, living arrangements, and social circles may feel unfamiliar, but they are also ripe for exploration!

How, you ask? Ditch the fear and embrace this as a adventure of self-discovery. Rediscover passions and dreams tucked away while raising kids. Encourage your adult children to do the same, reminding them that this is their chance to redefine themselves. You're all on this adventure together.

Acknowledge vulnerability and uncertainty with your adult children. Discuss hopes, fears, and questions. Sharing raw emotions fosters empathy and strengthens the bond. Open communication becomes your map for navigating this new landscape.

This transition, challenging as it may be, offers potential for personal growth and rediscovery. Embark on this journey with your adult children in a way that feels authentic to you—open your heart and embrace curiosity. A fulfilling new chapter awaits, even later in life.

Ripples and Waves: Beyond Family

Divorce impacts the immediate family and extends to the broader community—extended family, friends, and social circles. Navigating these relationships with sensitivity and open communication is crucial.

The impact on loved ones is not to be ignored. How might close friends react? How can you communicate your decision in a way that respects their feelings and addresses any concerns? They may need space to process this news and the impending change.

Consider financial aspects with your adult children. Focus on understanding your post-divorce financial requirements before dividing assets (Fuscaldo, 2022). Vent to trusted friends, family, or a therapist for mental clarity. Be open and honest about the changes your adult children might face, discussing potential impacts and exploring solutions. Transparency fosters trust and security.

Acknowledge the emotional rollercoaster your adult children are on. Validate their feelings, whether sadness, anger, confusion, or relief. Let them know it's okay to experience different emotions and offer unwavering support without judgment. Strengthen your bond and navigate this new chapter together by creating a safe space for open communication and understanding.

Supporting Their Journey: Launching Themselves

Watching your children grow into adults brings pride, but also uncertainty. They're charting their own course now, and your role as a parent shifts. The instinct to guide and protect remains, but the approach adapts to their independence to be successful.

Respect your adult children's autonomy. Offer support when needed but avoid making their decisions or taking sides in conflicts. Create space for them to learn, make mistakes, and build their own support networks. Encourage them to confide in friends, therapists, or support groups; healthy adult relationships don't mean solely relying on parents.

Encourage your adult children to share their thoughts and feelings, even when it's difficult. Actively listen to their joys and struggles, validate their emotions, and avoid defensiveness. This doesn't mean condoning every choice but creating a safe space for them to express themselves freely. They're not children seeking approval; they're adults seeking understanding and connection.

This transition is an opportunity to redefine your relationships with your adult children. Help them envision their future in terms of careers, aspirations, and their relationship with both parents. Encourage them to set healthy boundaries and communicate their needs. This might involve navigating tricky conversations about household roles, financial assistance, or extended family dynamics. Open communication is key to building healthy and respectful relationships.

If amicable co-parenting is possible, leverage a united front. Discuss shared values, communication approaches, and conflict-minimization strategies. Despite the breakup, you're still a team for your adult children's well-being. Working together provides stability and consistency during this phase.

Be patient, flexible, and adaptable. There will be adjustments and new dynamics. Don't let setbacks demotivate you; instead, celebrate small victories and rely on your support network.

If navigating these changes feels overwhelming, seek professional help. Therapists specializing in family transitions or divorce can offer invaluable guidance. A neutral third party can facilitate difficult conversations, manage emotions, and help you navigate individual and family dynamics more effectively.

Acknowledge the enduring love and connections you have with your adult children. Embrace the journey, celebrate their growth, and cherish the evolving bond.

Finding Joy and Growth After Later-Life Divorce

Divorce at any stage is tough, but later in life, it can be jarring. A life built together for decades ends, leaving you questioning your identity and future. Yet, through the emotional upheaval lies an unexpected gem: the opportunity for growth and discovery. This, my friend, is not your story's end but the exciting opening of your second act.

Reclaim neglected or suppressed parts of yourself. Rediscover old hobbies or explore new passions. Immerse yourself in creative pursuits, travel to dream destinations, or enjoy quiet introspection. This time is for exploration, redefinition, and creating a life that resonates with who you are now.

The "silver splitting" phenomenon is increasingly common, with rising divorces among older adults (Huff, 2023). This shared journey offers understanding and encouragement by connecting with others in similar transitions. Seek local groups, online forums, or therapy to share experiences and gain insights and encouragement.

It's important to acknowledge the challenges ahead: grief, financial concerns, and new family dynamics. However, each challenge is an opportunity for personal growth and resilience. Embrace life's adventure, savor milestones, and chart a course toward a future brimming with potential and optimism.

Life after divorce: How you can start again (2022) and Busco (2020) offers practical tips to navigate this exciting but daunting transition:

- Reconnect with yourself: Reflect on your values, interests, and dreams. What brings you joy and fulfillment?
- Build a strong support network: Surround yourself with positive, supportive people who believe in you.
- Step up, step out! Explore new interests, connect with others, and discover hidden possibilities.
- Seek professional guidance: consider therapy or financial planning services if you're struggling.
- Celebrate your journey: Acknowledge your successes, big and small, and embrace your unique path.

Your second act can be an extraordinary adventure filled with self-discovery, meaningful connections, and boundless possibilities. Embrace the unknown, stay positive, and write the next chapter of your story with joy and purpose.

Redefining Family: Blending New Chapters With Old Bonds

Life rarely follows an expected script, and sometimes, after years of raising your own family, you embark on a new chapter—a new love, a second marriage. These changes can shift the family landscape in unexpected ways, especially for your adult children. Your adult children have their own stories, feelings, and adjustments to make. Introduce your partner gradually, respecting their need to get comfortable with the new family dynamic before expecting a gushing welcome. Start with casual interactions, allowing everyone time to build rapport. Be patient, flexible, and open to compromise. Consider a family therapist as an ally in navigating complex dynamics.

Open communication is key. Talk openly with your adult children and reassure them that your new relationship doesn't diminish your love for them. Address their concerns honestly and with empathy. It builds trust and bridges the gap between uncertainty and understanding. Communication is complex. Negative communication doesn't always cause problems, and positive communication isn't always helpful. Focusing on relationship awareness might be beneficial (Karney & Bradbury, 2020).

"New" doesn't erase "old." Your original family bonds are precious, while your new partner adds a different ingredient. Embrace the evolving landscape instead of clinging to the past or forcing a picture-perfect image. Celebrate individual achievements within the new family unit, encouraging everyone to maintain their unique identities. A beautiful tapestry is woven from diverse threads, not forced uniformity.

Quality time is essential to any family recipe. Dedicate time for bonding with each person—your adult children, partner, and yourself. This fosters individual connections within the larger unit, preventing isolation. Plan shared activities, creating shared memories and togetherness. Celebrate holidays and traditions inclusively, accommodating everyone's preferences.

Respect individual boundaries and preferences, allowing space and interests. A healthy family is built on mutual respect and understanding, not forced conformity. Put yourself in your children's shoes. They may worry about their place in the family, their future, or their relationship with their partner. Offer empathy and validation without judgment, understanding that their adjustment takes time. Introduce your partner gradually, allowing them to get comfortable at their own pace. Building authentic relationships takes time and effort. Focus on connecting genuinely, letting connections develop organically.

Blending families is like creating a masterpiece; it takes experimentation, patience, and love. Celebrate every milestone, no matter how small. Maintain realistic expectations, understanding that blending isn't instant. Add relatable anecdotes to connect with others and address adult children's concerns with empathy. Touch on navigating finances when necessary. Include inspiring stories of successful blended families and provide resources like books, websites, or support groups. With the right ingredients and understanding, create a blend that nourishes everyone.

Navigating these transitions can be challenging, but it's an opportunity for growth. Reflect on your core values and intuition. Embrace imperfection, learn from stumbles, and celebrate victories. Share your story, inspire others, and live by example. Focus on what truly matters, invest in creating memories, fostering connections, and positively impacting those around you. This is your story, and you hold the power to write it with purpose, joy, and meaningful connections.

Embrace the unexpected, navigate the challenges, and discover the exciting possibilities in this new chapter.

Keeping the Lines Open: Importance of Communication in Later-Life Divorce

Communication is vital in a later-life divorce. Active listening, validation, and avoiding defensiveness are crucial for honest communication. The transition from divorce or separation is an opportunity to redesign relationships with adult children.

Your connection with your adult children and your role as a parent continues after a divorce. Prioritize open and honest communication to navigate this new chapter with understanding and support and rediscover the joy of connection in an evolving landscape.

This chapter has explored "silver splitting," guiding you through emotional waves, family dynamics, and empowering you to embrace growth and discovery within this transition. As you embark on this new chapter, reflect on the strategies presented and consider how to integrate them into your journey.

- Understand the "why." What factors contributed to your decision to divorce? Acknowledging your unmet needs, evolving priorities, and communication challenges can offer insights for navigating the present and shaping your future.
- What matters to you in this new chapter of your parental life?
- Are you ready to embrace the evolving family landscape, respect individual identities, and build new relationships with your adult children and potential new partners?
- Are you ready to step outside your comfort zone, rekindle old passions, or explore new hobbies for joy and fulfillment?
- How can you nourish your mind, body, and spirit through activities that promote well-being and personal growth?
- Are you open to the unexpected possibilities and exciting adventures in this new chapter of your life?

- What steps can you take to implement the strategies discussed in this chapter?
- What resources or support systems will you seek to navigate this journey?

This is your journey, and as you know by now, there's no one-size-fits-all approach. By integrating these strategies with your needs and desires, you can navigate this transition, embrace personal growth, and chart a course toward a fulfilling new chapter. By reflecting on these questions and tailoring the strategies to your situation, you can empower yourself to write a meaningful next chapter.

Chapter 4: Building Support for Adult Children

Plans change, detours happen, and the unexpected is often lurking around the next bend. For some families, life takes an unexpected turn, leading them down a path of challenges and triumphs. This chapter delves into the experiences of parents navigating these circumstances with their adult children, be it supporting someone through addiction or coping with disabilities. Here, we acknowledge the emotional rollercoaster parents embark on, offering tools and insights to empower their adult children while nurturing their well-being.

Imagine receiving news that alters your adult child's trajectory, shattering preconceived notions, and unleashing a wave of emotions. Denial, disbelief, and shock might numb you initially, making it difficult to process. Pain, guilt, disappointment, and anger might surface as reality sets in, leaving you feeling lost and overwhelmed. It's crucial to remember that these are valid parts of the healing process. Elisabeth Kübler-Ross's grief model (Tyrrell et al., 2023) provides a framework, reminding you that healing isn't linear. Be patient; within you lies immense strength and resilience.

Prioritize your emotional and spiritual stability before supporting your adult child. Focus on self-care practices that resonate with you. Taking care of yourself isn't selfish; it's the foundation for effective support for your adult child.

This journey is tough. Find insights and tools from experienced parents to foster independence, education, and social inclusion, unlocking your adult child's potential despite disabilities. Learn about navigating addiction, from identifying signs to offering support and understanding the path to recovery.

Knowledge, support, and self-care are your guiding lights. You're not just a caregiver but an individual with your own needs and aspirations. Don't neglect your passions and pursuits; they fuel your inner strength and allow you to show up for your adult child authentically.

As a parent, you can empower your adult child to thrive with dedication and grace. It's a work in progress, with joy, sorrow, struggle, and growth. Embrace the journey, celebrate victories, and learn from challenges.

Substance Abuse: First Steps to Recovery

Substance abuse often manifests in subtle shifts. Its effects reach deep into families, leaving confusion, hurt, disgrace, and helplessness. Navigating these waters is never easy. Recognizing early signs and steps toward recovery can feel like venturing into uncharted territory. With awareness and the right support, you can become your adult child's anchor.

Substance abuse affects families in numerous ways. Knowing the signs and symptoms is crucial for early intervention. These can manifest in various ways, depending on the individual. How do you spot the subtle shifts in your adult child's behavior? Changes in behavior can be revealing. Imagine their usual bubbly attitude being replaced by persistent negativity or sudden irritability. Their social circle might change as they withdraw from old friends, and a less-than-ideal crowd fills the void. Changes in appearance can be a sign; fatigue, personal care and hygiene changes, and unexplained weight loss or gain can be concerning. Losing interest in once-enjoyed activities or avoiding family gatherings can be a red flag. These small changes can be early indicators of a deeper issue.

Addressing this sensitive topic requires a delicate touch. Blame and shame only drag everyone down further. This journey is about love, understanding, and showing your adult child that you're their refuge, not a threat. Approach them with an open heart, expressing your concerns and desire to help without ultimatums or threats. You're on the same team, even if it feels like you're playing different games.

Family involvement is a powerful force in recovery. Your unwavering support significantly increases their chances of getting and staying healthy. You can join family support groups—safe spaces to connect with others who understand your struggles and offer guidance. Sharing experiences and finding strength in vulnerabilities can make a difference.

Balancing support and enabling can be challenging. Providing financial support for their addiction, even with good intentions, can hinder their progress by removing consequences and discouraging them from seeking help. Channel your resources towards empowering their recovery efforts through therapy, rehabilitation, and support groups. True love empowers, not enables. Supporting their active steps toward recovery gives them the strength and self-reliance to build a fulfilling life beyond addiction.

Setting boundaries is crucial, not punishment. It's about creating a healthy space for everyone. Be clear and firm about intolerable behaviors and consequences. Boundaries are for your adult child and for you. You need to take care of yourself to care for them. Consider joining a support group for caregivers, finding healthy outlets for stress, and asking for help.

This path won't be smooth. There will be stormy days, detours, and moments when you feel lost. But you're not alone. You can navigate this journey with knowledge, support, and unwavering love and understanding. It's about learning, growing, and finding a new way forward—where everyone thrives. So, take a deep breath and lean on your support system. You've got the strength and love to weather any storm. The journey may be long and unpredictable, but shared efforts can pave the way towards better days.

Substance abuse is often a symptom of deeper emotional or psychological struggles. As you support your adult child's recovery, addressing these underlying factors is crucial. This might involve exploring triggers like past trauma, stress, or mental health conditions. With therapy, your adult child can gain understanding, develop healthy coping mechanisms, and avoid substances. This exploration requires patience and empathy. It's about understanding the root causes and empowering your adult child to build resilience and emotional well-being. By addressing these factors, you're not just helping them overcome addiction but also fostering their overall emotional and mental health. Sincere, caring, and loving communication is vital.

Empowering Adult Children With Disabilities

Supporting an adult child with disabilities is intricate and multifaceted. It's a lifelong journey that demands unwavering love and a balance of support while fostering independence. Understanding diverse needs, nurturing self-sufficiency, exploring education and employment, and building strong social connections are vital to helping your adult child live a fulfilling life. Understanding your adult child's specific needs, strengths, and challenges is crucial for practical support. This requires active listening, lifelong learning, and seeking guidance from various sources. Interact with disability-specific communities and resources, connect with families facing similar experiences, and engage with professionals. Recognizing their life trajectory empowers you to become an informed advocate, tailoring your support to address their barriers and pave the way for success. This is about understanding their wishes and collaborating to build a future tailored to their aspirations.

Support your adult child's independence by encouraging them to develop life skills like managing finances, daily routines, public transportation, and hobbies. Celebrate their victories and increase their responsibilities as their confidence grows. Equip them with tools and confidence to do things for themselves, fostering accomplishment and self-sufficiency. Prioritize their self-sufficiency, knowing your support and guidance are always available.

Supporting your adult child's education and career goals unlocks possibilities. Explore inclusive programs that cater to their needs and learning styles. Advocate for accommodations and equal access to resources. Collaborate with career counselors and disability service providers to identify training and job placement. Their disability doesn't define their potential; their dreams deserve equal space. Encourage diverse career paths and equal opportunities to empower them. Employment statistics by the U.S. Bureau of Labor Statistics (2019) reveal insights into the experiences and barriers of individuals with disabilities. Understanding these statistics is crucial for effective support and advocating for equitable opportunities. Inclusion and opportunity are vital for success.

Human connection is essential for everyone, including individuals with disabilities. Encourage your adult child to engage with others who share similar experiences or interests, impacting their well-being. Encourage participation in community groups, support networks, or online forums. Celebrate their connections and help them navigate social interaction, combating isolation and fostering belonging. A solid social network empowers them to build relationships, develop communication skills, and navigate challenges with confidence and support. Connection is about having people around and creating a sense of belonging and shared understanding.

Supporting an adult child with disabilities demands love, patience, and a willingness to learn and adapt. Embrace these principles to become their advocate, empowering them to live fulfilling lives with independence and potential. Let your love guide them on their unique journey.

My friend, Patty, has experience supporting a young adult with developmental delays, including those on the autism spectrum, and shared valuable advice and encouragement for other families in similar circumstances. I hope you find it helpful:

- Preserve who you are. Maintain your identity and well-being while supporting your adult child.
- Learn to be in a relationship without giving yourself away. Find a balance between offering support and setting boundaries.
- Consider all living options for your adult child's needs and preferences.
- Know what's best for your family. Make decisions that consider everyone's well-being.
- Utilize available resources to support families with disabled individuals. Seek help and guidance without hesitation.
- It's an ongoing balancing act. Be prepared to adapt as your adult child's needs and circumstances change.
- Encourage your adult child to connect with others who share their interests and experiences to find their 'tribe' and enjoy themselves socially.
- Give them every opportunity to be safely independent. Support your adult child as they develop life skills and pursue independence.
- Employers can accommodate challenged adults. Consider inclusive workplaces.
- Lean on family and friends for support.
- Just do your best and be kind to yourself. Celebrate your efforts.

Keeping the Lines Open: Amidst Challenges and Satisfaction

Raising adult children with disabilities can be challenging and satisfying. Disabilities range from ADHD to various physical disabilities. Gathering information and finding support is helpful. There are many support groups, but sometimes people don't want to share their struggles. There are helpful books. Knowing we're not alone is important. It can help us and others in similar situations. Be open to encouragement and sharing it without claiming to have all the answers. Keep communicating, actively listening, and validating. Create a safe space for communication. Let them know they can come to you and that you are patient and understanding. Be willing to adapt your communication style based on their needs.

This chapter invites you to explore and discover. As you unpack the strategies, ask: How can they spark meaningful conversations between you and your adult child? Let these tools guide you towards new experiences and a deeper understanding of coping with disabilities:

- Reflect on the balance between support and independence. How can you encourage your adult child's self-sufficiency while still offering assistance?
- What resources or support systems could help you care for your adult child with special circumstances?
- Which substance abuse or disability strategy resonates with you and your current goals? Choose the one you're optimistic about implementing.
- Consider a recent communication challenge with your adult child. How could you have approached it differently using the tips in this chapter?
- Set a goal to foster your adult child's independence. How will you achieve it?
- Identify a support group or resource to connect with for guidance and community.
- How do societal perceptions of disabilities impact your interactions with your adult child?
- What are the unique challenges and strengths specific to your adult child's situation?
- How do you celebrate your adult child's individuality, achievements, and struggles?

- How can you create a safe space for open and honest family communication?
- Share a story about successfully navigating a communication challenge with your adult child.
- Imagine your adult child's ideal future. How can you help them achieve it?
- Write a letter to your adult child expressing love, understanding, and commitment to their journey.
- Reflect on your journey as a parent. What have you learned and grown from?

I hope this helps! Next, we explore how to navigate shifting dynamics.

Part 2: Navigate Shifting Dynamics

As your adult child charts their own course in life, the familiar landscape of your relationship undergoes a metamorphosis. Roles transform, and dynamics shift. Embarking on this exciting yet uncharted trajectory can be filled with joy and uncertainty. In the following pages, you will find guidance through these evolving family dynamics with clarity, compassion, and practical tools.

Imagine navigating the delicate symphony of financial responsibility with your adult child. This can be very challenging. Part of the challenge is offering strategies to empower them towards responsible financial management, fostering a harmonious balance between autonomy and the safety net of support you offer. Learn the delicate art of financial backing, striking the perfect balance between compassion and enabling to ensure resources contribute to their growth. By delving into sensitive conversations about contributions, estate planning, and establishing healthy boundaries, you can create a financial plan that resonates with both generations, building trust and mutual respect.

Whether you want to accept it or not, there is a generational divide between you and your adult child. Bridging the gap can sometimes feel like deciphering a foreign language. Be ready to explore the potential dissonance arising from differing values and perspectives. You will learn to comprehend the unique characteristics of your generation and your adult children, offering tools to bridge the communication gap and cultivate empathy. By understanding the "why" behind each other's perspectives, you can create mutual respect and understanding.

As your adult child journeys through career paths, relationships, and potentially parenthood, your role evolves. Reflecting on my journey as a parent and the changing dynamics of my relationship with my adult child, the image of a tandem bike comes to mind. The exhilarating yet sometimes scary feeling of relying on each other, the need for clear communication and coordinated effort to navigate turns, and the trust required when you can't see the road ahead – it all resonates deeply. It is your responsibility to provide guidance on adjusting to these changes, establishing healthy boundaries, and fostering new forms of support and connection. Imagine this chapter in your life as a choreographer, helping you transition to new roles within your family unit, ensuring your love and support remain the heart of the performance.

In your interactions with your adult child, you will definitely discover the crucial need to establish healthy boundaries in this yet to be written portion of your relationship. We discuss the importance of open communication, setting respectful limits, and fostering mutual understanding. By creating a clear "Boundary Blueprint," you can navigate potential conflicts with grace and this new dynamic with respect and independence, ultimately strengthening your relationship in the long run.

You are invited to embrace the tides of change with open arms. You can transform this transition into a beautiful masterpiece of growth and understanding by grasping the nuances of this evolving relationship, fostering open communication, and setting healthy boundaries. This new chapter in your familial journey can be a journey of love, respect, and unwavering support, offering opportunities to reconnect and build an even stronger bond with your adult child. Let your love guide you through your relationship's shifting dynamics while establishing a connection that resonates for years.

Navigating these transitions is a journey, not a destination. Embrace the unexpected twists, turns, and change of direction. Savor the moments with your adult child, and most importantly, allow the love between you to guide your thoughts, words, and actions.

Share Your Thoughts, Share the Love

Your Words Can Change Lives

"Helping others is the secret sauce to a happy life." - Karen M. Carlson

Thank you for reading this book. If you've found a little peace, a little understanding, or even a chuckle in these pages, imagine sharing that to help others. That's what we're here for, right? To make life a smidge easier for each other.

So, I've got a tiny but mighty favor to ask:

Would you mind sharing your thoughts on this book with folks who haven't discovered it yet? Think of it as passing on a little note of hope to a parent who might be pacing the floor at 2 a.m., wondering, "Am I doing this right?"

Our goal with "Peacefully Parenting Adult Children" is to bridge the gap between the hearts of our adult sons and daughters, whether they're just down the hall or across the country. Reaching those hearts far and wide can start with you.

Writing a review is easier than you think! It doesn't cost a penny and takes less than a minute, but your words could be the beacon of light someone desperately needs. Your review could help:

...a parent feel less alone in their struggles.

...a family find new ways to communicate.

...an empty-nester rediscover their purpose.

...an adult child see their parent in a new light.

...and so many more moments of connection and understanding.

Here's how to spread the love:

1.   Click on this QR code

2. Share your thoughts, feelings, and ah-ha moments. Wasn't that easy?

If lending a hand makes your heart happy, then you're definitely one of us! Welcome aboard the kindness train – there's always room for more.

I can't wait to dive back into sharing strategies, stories, and smiles with you.

Thank you a million times over. Your support means the world, not just to me, but to every parent out there searching for a little peace of mind.

- Your friend and fellow journeyer, Karen

P.S. - Remember, sharing is caring. If this book provided you a helpful nudge, consider passing it on to another parent in the wild. Who knows? You might just make their day (or night).

Chapter 5: Grown-Up Finances— Navigating Independence Together

Supporting our children's financial journey is challenging. The urge to shield them from hardship is strong, but genuine support empowers them. Balancing help and self-reliance is tricky. Providing too much assistance can hinder their growth while leaving them alone can lead to unnecessary struggles. How do we avoid enabling dependence?

This journey to financial independence requires a shift in perspective. We need to see challenges as learning and growth opportunities instead of problems. This chapter will guide you through this process, offering strategies to empower your adult child toward financial self-sufficiency.

Financial freedom involves the resources, skills, and confidence to manage them effectively. We'll equip you to support your adult child to foster trust, resilience, and long-term financial stability by exploring setting boundaries, open communication, budgeting, and navigating obstacles. The goal is not to control but to provide guidance and encouragement for independence. By fostering responsible habits early on, you empower your adult child to make informed decisions.

Navigating the "Bank of Mom and Dad"

When adult children leave home, the issue of supporting them without enabling them arises. Statistics show that nearly a third of Millennials and Gen Zers over 18 receive financial support from their parents (Dickler, 2022). Over 50% of young adults in the U.S. rely on it (Barroso et al., 2019). This affects career choices, living situations, and self-reliance. Lending money to adult children can foster independence or hinder it. The key is differentiating between one-off support and promoting reliance on the "Bank of Mom and Dad."

The "Bank of Mom and Dad" may seem tempting, but clear boundaries and open communication are essential. You may give your adult child money without expecting repayment but consider using loans with accountability-promoting terms. Open and honest conversations about expectations, needs, and financial goals are crucial. Set up regular family meetings for transparent financial discussions. It's guidance and support, not prying. Supporting your adult child financially requires balancing responsibility and help, building trust, and ensuring an understanding of loan vs. gift implications. Consider the potential impact. Lending money should maintain your financial stability.

Consider your adult child's creditworthiness, urgency, and repayment ability. Be honest about your concerns and ensure they have a realistic repayment plan. Formalize the agreement with a written document to solidify expectations and protect both parties. Financial freedom empowers your child to manage their finances independently. Choose the path that best helps them achieve that goal without compromising your well-being.

My experience as a child who didn't receive money gifts has shaped my approach to helping my adult children. When I was a young adult, my parents provided money for unexpected needs with a clear repayment plan, which was appreciated. I continued this with my children, and it worked well. Treating them as adults sets clear expectations.

Mastering financial basics early helps you make informed decisions later in life. These skills become crucial for those entering or recently graduating from post-secondary education as responsibilities and financial exposure increase (RBC Wealth Management, 2024). Setting boundaries means establishing healthy parameters that promote independence and responsible financial management. While patience and understanding are essential, enforce the financial boundaries with compassion for adult children struggling with self-regulation. This enables them to experiment and make mistakes without fear of judgment. Let's look at the necessary skills for your adult child.

Modeling Good Habits: Learning by Example

Use transparency as a teaching tool. Help your adult child set budgets, explore saving and investment options, manage credit scores, file taxes, save for retirement, and access resources like Investopedia, NerdWallet, TurboTax, or budgeting apps. Share your budgeting strategies, retirement plans, and how you make financial decisions. If uncomfortable, suggest a financial planner.

Not all children learn best from their parents, and that's okay. Consider alternative avenues like coaches, mentors, or planners. Sometimes participating in group coaching adds to the "safety in numbers" dynamic while feeling the support of others in similar circumstances.

I recently connected with a money mindset coach, Jessica Kleine (2024). I know I'm never too old to learn new strategies for money management. Here is what she said: When modeling good habits, I would avoid saying, "Do what I say, not what I do." I feel like that's what becomes the default response. We want to teach our kids to be better than we are, but that means we need to be mindful of the kind of example we are setting. We can't just teach them to be better with money if we're not willing to do better ourselves. We can talk about it until we're blue in the face, but if they don't see us doing what we're trying to teach them, it won't stick. So really, to lead our children to a better financial future, we need to head that way ourselves first.

Saying "No" With Compassion

Saying "no" to a financial request is tough, but honesty and compassion are crucial for a healthy relationship. It's natural to want to say yes, but sometimes, saying no is the most loving and responsible action. Let your adult child know you understand their situation and emotions, validate their feelings, and express empathy. Saying, "I see how much this is impacting you, and I care," can alleviate the sting of rejection. Then, explain your reasons honestly. Share your financial limitations or concerns clearly, such as saving for retirement, unforeseen expenses, or the inability to afford the requested amount. You don't need to justify your decision beyond a straightforward explanation. It's important to emphasize that saying "no" doesn't diminish your love and support. You can still offer emotional support. A strong parent adult-child relationship transcends finances.

Holding on to negative emotions creates distance and tension. Strive for open communication and find solutions that benefit both of you. Your relationship is more valuable than any financial decision. Saying "no" can guide your adult child toward financial independence with compassion, honesty, and a focus on maintaining a healthy connection.

Financial Struggles: Guiding Toward Independence

Life's unexpected detours often lead to financial struggles for adult children, triggering a strong instinct in parents to protect them from hardship. However, genuine support is the catalyst for empowering them to build a solid financial foundation for their long-term success. Researchers have found that many believe parents often do too much for their young adult children (Barroso et al., 2019). They also emphasize the importance of finding a balance between assistance and guidance toward self-reliance. Offering occasional support during tough times is okay, but avoid hindering their growth or creating dependency. Before offering solutions, delve into the reasons behind their struggles. Listen to their concerns, acknowledge their challenges, and explore the underlying factors. This strengthens your bond and ensures your support addresses their specific needs.

Encouraging financial independence requires establishing a strong foundation. Achieving financial stability is not a straightforward journey. There will be unexpected turns, setbacks, and moments of uncertainty. Empower them with knowledge. Remember, you're supporting them as they explore their own financial empowerment. One approach to accomplish this is by assisting adult children in creating practical budgets that align with their income and expenses. Instead of simply giving them money, consider helping them find ways to earn income by assisting with job applications, connecting them with financial aid resources, or brainstorming additional ways to make money. If your adult child lives at home, having them contribute to household expenses encourages responsibility and independence, preparing them for future living arrangements. Using financial management apps and tools can further enhance their control and transparency over their finances. Encourage your adult children to engage in resources such as financial literacy workshops, online courses, or seek guidance from a financial advisor for personalized support. Teaching them proactive financial planning techniques empowers them to anticipate expenses and allocate savings for unexpected emergencies, enabling them to address financial challenges with confidence and fortitude.

To address the overwhelming burden of student loan debt, consider strategies that promote self-sufficiency. While the desire to provide financial relief is strong, and offering temporary relief through co-signing on a consolidation loan may seem beneficial, it's important to establish clear repayment expectations to avoid complicating matters in the future. Open communication about expectations creates a solid foundation for navigating the balance between support and self-reliance, promoting your child's long-term financial well-being, and fostering a respectful relationship. Assisting with interest payments can alleviate the immediate financial strain. Encourage your adult children to take proactive steps towards tackling the principal amount. By equipping them with the necessary tools and knowledge to navigate these challenges independently, you help them build resilience and confidence for their financial journey ahead. These practices not only promote financial awareness but also empower them to make well-informed decisions about their priorities and navigate future challenges independently.

Your role extends beyond providing resources and guidance. Maintaining open communication with your adult children is key to promoting financial independence. Let your adult child know they are not alone on this journey. Showing active listening, validating their emotions, and avoiding judgment are crucial aspects of building trust and offering personalized support. Provide unwavering emotional support. Celebrating their achievements—no matter how small—and recognizing their efforts helps reinforce the importance of self-reliance and encourages them to persevere in their financial pursuits. Your love, guidance, and belief in their abilities are powerful motivators.

Keeping the Lines Open: Discuss the Money

Communication is crucial for support and empowerment. Open and honest conversations create a safe space for your adult child to voice their goals, concerns, and anxieties. Actively listen without judgment, offering empathy and understanding. Collaborate on solutions, fostering a sense of ownership and responsibility. Prioritizing communication builds trust and forges a deeper connection, strengthening the foundation for financial independence.

Consider how to support and help your adult child. Reflect on your journey and relationship.

- What are your hopes for your adult child's financial future and your role in their journey?
- Assess your current financial support practices. Do you provide financial assistance to your adult child? If so, how do you offer it? (loans, gifts, covering expenses)?
- Evaluate your communication style. Do you discuss finances openly with your adult child? Are you comfortable discussing your financial situation?
- How confident is your adult child in budgeting, managing debt, and planning for the future?
- Create a financial vision board to depict your adult child's financial future and your role in supporting them. Share and discuss the boards.
- Create a "Financial Support Agreement."

Money matters, as does fostering independence and resilience. By integrating these insights, you can support your adult child without enabling dependence. The goal is to empower them toward financial independence and build a lasting relationship based on mutual understanding and support.

Celebrate your adult child's financial successes, no matter how small. Acknowledge their efforts and resilience to reinforce their confidence and motivation. Offer emotional support during setbacks, but guide them towards solutions to foster their inner strength and resourcefulness. Prioritize communication, empowerment, and unwavering support to equip your adult child with the tools for financial independence and cultivate a lasting bond.

Chapter 6: Bridging Time— Understanding the Generational Divide

In our fast-paced world, where technology advances rapidly and societal norms constantly shift, navigating family relationships can feel like scaling Mount Everest in flip-flops—exhilarating and unstable. One significant challenge for parents lies in bridging the gap with their adult children, whose generations are shaped by contrasting experiences and perspectives. This generational divide offers both hurdles and opportunities, and this guide delves into practical tools to foster connection and understanding.

The laughter around the once-familiar childhood dinner table holds a new undercurrent. Your adult child sits across the table, laughter punctuated by financial burdens and career uncertainties. This is the reality for many families today as adult children return home due to socioeconomic factors. Student loan debt and a competitive job market play a significant role, but cultural variations exist. Navigating this phenomenon requires redefining boundaries, adapting expectations, and fostering mutual respect. Open and honest conversations about responsibilities, financial contributions, and lifestyle needs can help strike a balance.

Fostering connection goes beyond bridging the gap. Embracing the generational divide as a natural part of societal evolution instead of a barrier opens doors to learning and growth. Imagine your parents, once bewildered by your clothes and music, now seeking your insights on social media trends and cryptocurrency. Can you imagine what your adult child must be thinking? Seeing differences as opportunities for dialogue and enrichment is crucial. This journey requires an open mind, a willingness to embrace empathy and continuous learning. Imagine listening to your adult child's thoughts and feelings without judgment. Picture engaging in respectful dialogue, acknowledging differing viewpoints without defensiveness, and creating a space for genuine exchange. Finding common ground despite the divide means building upon shared values, interests, or experiences, like a love of music, a family recipe, or a shared cause.

The generational gap can be a connection, growth, and a strengthened bond between parent and adult child. Exploring the complexities of connecting with adult children across generations, examining conflict strategies, and emphasizing the importance of maintaining healthy relationships and promoting overall well-being can be exhilarating.

Adapting to Living With Adult Children

The rise of "boomerang children" is a modern trend where adult children move back home for various reasons (Mangrum et al., 2022). This trend requires parents to redefine boundaries, adjust expectations, and foster mutual respect. Strategies supporting independence while sharing space are essential for a healthy dynamic.

In 2022, the U.S. Census Bureau reported that 16.3% of young adults aged 25–34 lived with their parents (United States Census Bureau, 2022), highlighting an increasing trend. This trend offers a chance for renewed connection but requires adjustments. Redefine boundaries, adapt expectations, and foster mutual respect. Empower your adult child's independence while sharing space. Support their job search, encourage financial planning, and respect their privacy, especially regarding relationships. Provide resources for job platforms, facilitate financial discussions, and offer your home as a haven, not an intrusion. Embrace generational differences, foster open communication, and adapt boundaries for a stronger relationship with your adult child. It is also important that your own privacy and freedom are allowed to flourish in this new relationship dynamic.

Embracing the Gap: Beyond Bridging, Understanding, and Growth

Recognizing the generation gap as a natural part of societal evolution is crucial. Each generation has its own unique societal and cultural context, leading to different perspectives. It's important for parents to understand, or at least be open to, their adult children's viewpoints, have open conversations, and model healthy disagreements. By embracing generational differences, both parents and adult children can foster growth and learning. Throughout history, each generation has had distinct values and beliefs. While differences may exist, it's crucial to see them as opportunities for learning and growth.

Embracing this journey requires openness, empathy, and a willingness to learn from each other, ultimately strengthening the bond between you and your adult child. Discovering the unique characteristics of different generations, learning effective communication strategies, and exploring practical techniques for bridging the generational gap with understanding are essential.

Our adult children navigate a different world. Embracing their perspectives gives us insights into our future. Each generation inherits values and biases. We have to examine our preconceptions and consider new perspectives. When you are presented with your adult child's viewpoint, question your assumptions about career paths, technology use, and social norms.

Blending experience with youth creates an environment for innovation and growth. Imagine brainstorming environmental solutions with your tech-savvy adult child or discussing social justice. The generational gap becomes a springboard for problem-solving and change; a source of creativity, driving progress and shaping a better future, allowing for innovative solutions, and challenging societal norms.

Mentorship: Bridging Generational Divides

Imagine a relationship based on mutual learning, open communication, and shared experiences, transcending generations, and strengthening family bonds. Parent-child mentorship fosters a vibrant exchange. Adult children gain insights from their parents' life journeys, navigating career choices, personal challenges, and lessons. Parents stay engaged with the modern world and learn fresh perspectives from their adult children, adapting to evolving trends and gaining new skills.

The benefits extend beyond skills and knowledge. This mentorship tackles generational divides. Stereotypes and misunderstandings create tension, but open communication and shared experiences bridge this gap. Parents share life lessons and cultural heritage, while adult children offer their views. This interaction fosters respect, empathy, and a deeper appreciation for each other's perspectives.

This approach extends beyond the immediate family, strengthening the community by offering a model for positive intergenerational connections. Parents share career advice with their adult children, mentor them in professional networks, or collaborate on entrepreneurial ventures. Adult children can guide their parents into the digital world or share social media marketing expertise. This reciprocal relationship fosters understanding, enriches lives, and bridges the generation gap, creating a stronger community.

Consider the transformative power of parent adult-child mentorship over traditional parenting. Witnessing the growth and understanding it fosters will strengthen your family bond and contribute to a more connected community. Rewrite the parent adult-child relationship narrative, showing that learning, growth, and support can flow both ways, creating a stronger, more loving family unit for generations.

Breaking Down Generational Stereotypes

The harm of generational stereotypes cannot be overstated. Instead of portraying parents as stuck and adult children as entitled, consider the talented adult child dismissed as inexperienced or the parent's life lessons dismissed as old-fashioned. These labels create walls, hindering communication and understanding.

The loss goes beyond missed opportunities. When we move beyond labels and engage in genuine connection, a beautiful exchange unfolds. It's an experience where parents and adult children grow and benefit. Dismantling stereotypes requires an active effort. Let's listen to each other's stories, set aside assumptions, and embrace each generation's experiences and perspectives. It's always helpful to create safe spaces for open communication where vulnerabilities are shared, and both parties express their needs and concerns. Finally, it's important to celebrate the individual strengths and talents of each family member, fostering mutual respect and appreciation.

We can build stronger parent adult-child relationships by moving beyond generational labels and embracing individual experiences. It's time to rewrite the family dynamic based on understanding, respect, and the shared journey of life. Only then can we unlock the potential for connection, growth, and love within every family, regardless of age.

Navigating Conflict: Communication and Professional Support

Conflict strategies in parent adult-child relationships significantly impact well-being. Active strategies used by parents contrast with passive ones, contributing to higher depressive symptoms.

Texting can lead to miscommunication among generations. When my adult children and their spouses don't respond, I may assume something is wrong, but I've learned to communicate my needs calmly. For instance, I ask for a thumbs-up emoji or a brief response to confirm they've seen the text. I understand everyone is busy, so I try to avoid creating unnecessary assumptions. Open communication and clear expectations are essential. It's a reminder to approach conflicts with understanding and patience.

Seeking professional support, active listening, "I" statements, common ground, and empathy are valuable for navigating conflicts. Now that we recognize the gap as an opportunity let's explore conflict resolution strategies:

During conflicts, prioritize active listening. Understand your adult child's perspective without interrupting or making assumptions. Reflecting on their thoughts and feelings shows understanding and validation. Use "I" statements to express feelings instead of accusatory language for nonviolent communication.

Finding an agreement can help people connect during conflicts. You can start resolving differences by focusing on common interests or values. Empathy is crucial in understanding your adult child's emotions and motivations, fostering compassion despite disagreements.

When emotions are high, it's important to take a break and revisit the conversation when both parties are calmer to prevent escalation and thus create a more productive environment. If conflicts persist, seeking professional help from a family therapist or counselor can provide guidance, communication techniques, and support in navigating family dynamics.

During disagreements, prioritize understanding your adult child's perspective without interrupting. Reflecting on their thoughts and feelings shows validation. After one person speaks, summarize before offering your perspective. This reduces miscommunication. Managing emotions is crucial. Engage in activities like deep breathing, walking, or calming techniques to create space for communication.

Establishing conflict resolution ground rules is essential. These should promote respectful communication, including avoiding personal attacks, staying on topic, and taking turns speaking without interruption. Instead of seeking a resolution right away, prioritize understanding each other's perspectives and feelings to create empathy and find common ground.

Practice mindful communication by being fully present and engaged. Use mindfulness to stay focused on each other's words and nonverbal cues. Embrace forgiveness, as conflicts are natural. Let go of resentment and past grievances to build a stronger relationship. You can't accomplish mindful communication when one party is distracted or engaged with their mobile device!

Not all strategies apply to every situation, so choose the best for your circumstances and relationship dynamics. Conflict is natural in relationships, and our response to it matters. Seek professional support to navigate conflicts with your adult child constructively and respectfully.

Keeping the Lines Open: Discussing the Generational Divide

Effective communication is essential to understanding the generational divide. It allows for open conversations, exchanging viewpoints, and fostering empathy. Communication enables parents and adult children to bridge the gap, navigate conflicts, and build stronger relationships through active listening, respectful dialogue, and a willingness to learn.

This guide is your starting point. Reflect on your experiences and how they shape your relationship with your adult child.

- Reflect on your experiences and perspectives shaped by your generation. How do these differences affect your relationship with your adult child?
- What topics and how do you navigate differences in a conversation with your adult child about expectations and boundaries?
- How can you use shared interests or values to connect with your adult child?
- Reflect on a conflict with your adult child. How could active listening, "I" statements, and seeking common ground have helped potentially resolve it better?
- How do you approach conflicts with your adult child, especially in modern communication like texting?
- How can you prioritize active listening and nonviolent communication during conflicts with your adult child?
- How do you foster empathy for your adult child's emotions and motivations, even when you disagree?
- Can you establish ground rules with your adult child to promote respectful communication during conflicts?
- How can you practice mindful communication and forgiveness when navigating conflicts with your adult child?

Bridging the generational divide requires understanding and adapting to the dynamics of relationships with adult children. It involves recognizing generational differences, embracing open communication, and navigating conflicts with empathy and effective strategies. Parents can strengthen connections with their adult children, foster healthier relationships, and promote family harmony.

Chapter 7: New Roles and Responsibilities

As parents, we know that raising children is dynamic and ever-changing. We adapt and navigate the challenges, from sleepless nights of infancy to turbulent teenage years. But what catches us off guard is the transition to parenting adult children.

In this chapter, we explore new roles and responsibilities as our children enter adulthood, marking a significant shift in the parent adult-child relationship. We will discover that being excessively involved and in control is detrimental to a healthy relationship with your adult child. There are better ways to adapt your parenting style. It requires us to reassess our roles as guides, coaches, mentors, and supporters. As our child grows, our relationship also grows, and it's essential to understand this evolving landscape. We'll look at the importance of setting boundaries while offering guidance and support and provide strategies for nurturing healthy relationships with our adult children.

With open minds, patience, and adaptability, we can create a fulfilling relationship with our adult children. Together, we'll navigate this new territory and discover the joy and rewards of embracing our roles as parents of adult children.

Avoiding the Helicopter Parenting Trap

Helicopter parents exhibit excessive control and involvement in their children's lives, preventing them from developing autonomy. They lack trust in their child's capabilities, leading to over-reliance on parental guidance.

Recognizing the consequences of overparenting, particularly with adult children, is crucial for fostering independence and growth. Adults raised by helicopter parents may struggle with decision-making, problem-solving, and taking risks due to constant parental control and intervention, leading to a lack of self-reliance and feelings of inadequacy or low self-worth. The controlling behavior of helicopter parents can strain relationships with their adult children and hinder healthy interactions with peers, creating barriers to trust and mutual respect.

Parents may experience fears and uncertainties during this phase as they question their readiness to let go and allow their adult children to face the challenges of the world on their own. Seeking guidance through resources, books, or professional support like therapy or parenting workshops can provide valuable insights and strategies for navigating the challenges of parenting adult children. Parents can offer guidance and support from a mentoring perspective, finding a balance between providing advice and respecting their adult children's choices.

Finding New Ways to Connect: Beyond Overparenting

Parents can forge deeper connections with their adult children by embracing new approaches beyond helicopter parenting. Finding ways to connect starts with adapting parenting styles to become a supportive presence rather than a controlling force. This requires continuous effort and commitment. It's not about discarding previous parenting strategies but adapting to evolving relationship needs. It means letting go of control, embracing vulnerability, and trusting your adult child's ability to navigate their own life. By showing genuine interest in your adult children's lives, passions, and goals, parents can establish a stronger connection. Respecting personal boundaries is paramount. It allows adult children to define their identities and make choices. Parents can offer guidance and support while granting their children the freedom to navigate their paths. This doesn't mean abdicating responsibility. It's about shifting from dictates to guidance, offering wisdom and support without judgment. By fostering a relationship built on trust, respect, and support, parents can create an environment for mutual learning and growth. It creates a safe space for honest dialogue, where adult children feel respected and empowered to discuss their perspectives without fear of judgment or disapproval.

Let's look closer at what it means to be a guide, coach, mentor, and supporter of your adult child. By now, you know that your role as a parent of an adult child has changed. While the parent-child dynamic remains, navigating the shifting roles within the parent adult-child relationship is essential. Find the balance between providing support and guidance while respecting your adult children's autonomy.

As a guide, you offer wisdom and perspective, drawing on your life experiences to illuminate their path. You share lessons learned, highlighting potential pitfalls and celebrating successes. The challenge lies in striking a balance between guidance and overstepping. Offer support without imposing your will, allowing them to make their own choices and learn from their experiences.

A coach believes in your adult child's potential and helps unlock it. You encourage them to set goals, identify their strengths and weaknesses, and develop strategies for achievement. The challenge lies in avoiding the temptation to take over. Be their supporter, not their micromanager, fostering their self-reliance and intrinsic motivation.

Mentorship offers a unique opportunity to share knowledge and expertise in a specific area. This could be related to your career, hobbies, or life skills. The challenge lies in ensuring the chosen area aligns with your adult child's interests and avoiding unsolicited advice. Offer expertise when genuinely sought, fostering autonomy, and respecting their individual path.

You stand by your adult child, offering unwavering emotional support no matter what life throws your way. You listen without judgment, celebrate their victories, and provide a safe space during struggles. The challenge lies in setting healthy boundaries and avoiding enabling behaviors. Offer support that empowers them to overcome challenges, not one that hinders their growth and resilience.

These roles are not exclusive, and you may embody different ones at different times, sort of like wearing a different hat for a particular circumstance. The key is to be mindful of your adult child's needs and adjust your approach accordingly. Embrace continuous learning, open communication, and respect for their individuality.

Learning and Growing Together: A Continual Process

As parents, it's important to recognize that parenting doesn't end when our children become adults. It evolves and adapts to the changing dynamics of our relationships. Continually be open to learning from our adult children and growing alongside them, embracing the new insights and understanding they bring. Exploring interests and having stimulating conversations creates opportunities for continual personal and relational development. However, it also brings the value of vulnerability and authenticity to the relationship.

Vulnerability allows for genuine and deep connections to form. When parents are willing to be vulnerable, they open themselves up to their adult child, sharing insecurities, struggles, and emotions. This vulnerability creates a safe and non-judgmental space for the adult child to also share their vulnerabilities, fostering mutual understanding and empathy. It creates a sense of emotional closeness and authenticity in the relationship, allowing for a deeper level of connection.

Authenticity is essential to establishing trust and mutual respect in the parent adult-child relationship. When parents communicate and act authentically, they show that they are true to themselves and their values. This allows the adult child to perceive their parent as a genuine person, with hopes, fears, and imperfections. It fosters an environment of honesty and transparency, where both parties feel comfortable being their true selves. I know the mistakes I've made, and sometimes sharing them can help adult children realize we are all growing, learning, and changing.

Vulnerability and authenticity pave the way for continual growth and personal development. When parents are open about their journey of self-discovery, they show their adult child that changes and learning are a lifelong process. It encourages the adult child to embrace their growth and explore their unique path. By modeling vulnerability and authenticity, parents can inspire their adult children to strive for authenticity in their own lives, fostering personal growth and a sense of purpose.

All parent adult-child relationships are bound to have some tension. Birditt et al. (2009) found that not all tensions in parental relationships are equal. In their study, both parents and adult children reported feeling more stressed by individual concerns like finances and health than the overall relationship dynamic. However, families with adult children experienced higher conflict, possibly due to differing expectations. Importantly, the study found that tensions related to how families interact had a larger impact on overall relationship quality than individual concerns. This suggests that prioritizing clear communication and understanding each other's needs is crucial for maintaining strong parent adult-child bonds throughout life, regardless of the specific challenges that arise.

Relationships with adult children evolve. Each child requires a different approach, and some connections may be closer than others. Addressing conflicts constructively is important. It creates a sense of psychological safety within the relationship, where both parents and adult children feel heard, understood, and valued. Along with this, cultivating an atmosphere of forgiveness, understanding, and acceptance nurtures a bond for continued growth. This journey requires consistent effort, patience, and dedication to understanding and supporting one another.

Keeping the Lines Open: Stay Grounded

In this chapter, you have learned that staying grounded is important in parenting. Being grounded in your parenting addresses any anxiety you might have about your parenting role. Therefore, you can cultivate strong family relationships and refine essential skills by promoting open and healthy communication. It's important to remember that we are all humans and fail at times. How do we respond to that? We can acknowledge what we learned from the experience for our own benefit and possibly the benefit of our adult children.

Finding a balance between care and control and creating an environment that encourages open dialogue and honesty is paramount. Establishing a communication foundation rooted in respect and understanding fosters openness to feedback.

- How would you describe your approach to parenting your adult child? Are you more inclined toward controlling or being supportive? Why?

- Consider a recent interaction with your adult child. How did your communication style influence the outcome of the conversation? Did you approach it with openness and understanding, or did you default to a controlling or judgmental tone?
- Explore any anxieties or fears you may have about your adult child's choices or decisions. What underlying beliefs or values contribute to these anxieties? How can you address and work through them to create a more grounded and supportive mindset?
- Practice active listening with your adult child. You are welcome to go to Chapter 2 again and read "Active Listening: Tuning In to Truly Connect" to remind you about active listening. Choose a topic or issue they are passionate about and engage in a conversation where your main focus is to listen and understand their perspective without interrupting or offering advice. Reflect on the experience and how it made you feel.
- Look for opportunities to share your vulnerabilities and struggles with your adult child. Share a personal story or experience that illustrates your growth and learning. Discuss how it impacted your relationship and foster a deeper understanding.
- Schedule regular check-ins with your adult child to discuss goals, challenges, and areas where they may need guidance or support. Approach these conversations with a mindset of curiosity and mutual learning rather than control or judgment.
- Commit to self-reflection and personal growth as a parent. Reflect on your values and beliefs and how they influence your relationship with your adult child.

By staying grounded in your approach to parenting, you can build a strong foundation for a healthy and fulfilling relationship.

Chapter 8: Establishing New Boundaries

This chapter emphasizes the importance of boundaries in the relationship with adult children. So far, you have learned that setting healthy boundaries is crucial for maintaining respectful relationships and navigating changing family dynamics, especially in divorce, disabilities, substance abuse, and financial independence. Respecting their autonomy and individuality while being supportive is key.

Parental roles shift as children become adults, blurring the lines between parent and child as they navigate their lives and make decisions. This transition is exciting and challenging as we balance guidance with respect for their autonomy. Establishing new boundaries in the parent adult-child relationship is essential for a strong and secure relationship while allowing independence. Effective communication is crucial, as well as adapting the dynamics to express expectations and concerns while actively listening to their perspectives and respecting boundaries.

In this chapter, we'll explore setting new boundaries and open communication for a healthy relationship with our adult children. We'll learn to redraw lines with love, understanding, and respect while building strategies to navigate challenges and changes while preserving familial ties.

The Gradual Shift: Rigid to Fluid Interactions

As your child, who once needed bedtime stories, becomes an independent adult, parental control diminishes, giving way to individual decision-making and responsibility. This inevitable shift brings a subtle yet significant change in the parent-child relationship: boundaries blur. Clear lines—curfews, chore charts, and spoonfuls of peas—gradually fade, replaced by a more subtle and collaborative relationship.

This evolution can be unsettling. Suddenly, letting go after years of guiding and managing feels strange, even threatening. Bedtime stories are replaced by late-night calls about career changes, and chore charts become discussions about budgeting for shared vacations. It's natural to yearn for control, but clinging to rigid boundaries hinders growth and undermines trust built over years of love and nurturing.

The good news is that it doesn't mean surrendering completely. It means becoming supportive partners rather than authoritative figures. This transition can be challenging, requiring open communication and adaptability. Discussing financial decisions, offering guidance without dictating, and respecting their choices foster mutual trust and respect in this new phase.

Boundaries protect and nurture healthy relationships. As your child grows up, redefine those boundaries as bridges of communication, support, and unwavering love. This shift takes time, effort, and a healthy dose of letting go, but the reward is a mature, connected relationship built on mutual respect and understanding, allowing you to witness and celebrate their journey as an adult.

Acknowledge that this transition isn't linear. There will be moments of stepping back and seeking your guidance. Adapt, listen openly, and communicate effectively to establish evolving boundaries alongside your ever-changing relationship. You're not relinquishing control; you're transitioning to a different, yet equally fulfilling, role.

This shift in boundaries is a natural and necessary part of the parent-child relationship as children grow into adulthood. It requires effort for parents to navigate this transition and redefine their roles and interactions. Acknowledging this shift as normal can help parents establish new, healthier boundaries while respecting their adult children's autonomy while maintaining a strong connection.

Redrawing the Lines: Establishing New Boundaries

As teenagers grow older, the transition towards independence and establishing boundaries can happen at different ages and stages for each individual. This transition is influenced by factors like personality, maturity, life experiences, and cultural influences, not to mention their friends and peers. It's important to pay attention to your teenager's maturity and readiness for increased independence. This will guide your approach to setting boundaries and promoting their growth and autonomy.

As your child enters their 20s, they navigate higher education, career paths, and identity formation. Dating and life paths become significant. In their 30s, they prioritize career advancement, long-term partnerships, and potentially starting a family. Financial goals like homeownership and travel become priorities. By their 40s, their careers stabilize or evolve, children may be raised, and they may start caring for you or other family members. Personal growth through education and pursuing new interests persists during this phase.

Understanding the stages of adulthood can help you set boundaries to support your adult child's independence. Letting go may be tough at first, but communication and decision-making are important despite parental anxieties. Prioritizing your adult child's choices, valuing resilience, and embracing unconditional love through support and affirmation are key aspects of this process. This journey of mutual growth and learning demands adaptation and faith, changing both you and your adult child.

It's important to recognize that today's young adults are entering adulthood around five years later than previous generations (Steinberg, 2023). The concept of adulthood has evolved. Today's young adults are waiting longer to marry, buy homes, or build careers compared to previous generations. This trend, due to factors like rising education costs and delayed financial stability, means judging them solely based on where "their parents were at their age" can be misleading and inaccurate. You might be pleasantly surprised to find that your adult child is achieving similar things at their age, or perhaps even more! So let go of the generational comparison game and celebrate your adult child's progress on their own unique timeline.

In navigating this transition, it is crucial to recognize and respect the growing autonomy of your adult children in order to maintain strong family ties. Engaging in family traditions is important. It fosters connection, identity, and belonging for both parents and adult children, shaping a healthy sense of self from a young age and providing a foundation for personal growth as children transition into adulthood. By participating in family traditions, you strengthen family ties and cultivate lasting trust with your adult child.

It's important to actively listen to your adult child to strengthen your relationship. This means showing genuine interest in their thoughts, feelings, and experiences. As your child transitions into adulthood, it's important to maintain open dialogue and encourage honest communication without placing blame, even in moments of mistake or error. Embracing active listening fosters trust and compassion, which lays the groundwork for connectedness and positive influence. Listen without interrupting, acknowledge their feelings, offer sincere praise, share your flaws openly, respect their opinions, and be receptive to their feedback. This creates a safe space for honest conversations and deeper connections. Building strong communication with your adult child requires respecting their time and opinions. Avoid offering unsolicited advice, rudeness, quick fixes, gossip, guilt trips, anger, and manipulation when your desires aren't met. Express disappointment respectfully and maintain empathy. Adult children are independent individuals.

Boundaries set at one point may need adjustments as your adult child transitions through life. By embracing this ongoing process, you can navigate the complexities of the parent adult-child relationship and create a strong foundation for a healthy and fulfilling connection.

Communicating Boundaries: Dialogue, Not Monologue

Talking to your adult child about setting boundaries can be tough. To encourage your adult child to open up, consider engaging in activities together that you both enjoy. Spending quality time together and creating positive experiences can help build a comfortable and relaxed environment for open communication. However, it's important not to dive into personal topics right away. Instead, start with lighter subjects and gradually delve deeper into more personal discussions over time. Building a habit of regular, open conversation can strengthen your connection and encourage your adult child to feel more comfortable sharing their thoughts and feelings with you. When you have the conversation, show confidence.

Clear boundaries help navigate conflict, avoid codependency, and be mindful of your and your adult child's mental health and emotional well-being. When you establish new boundaries, approach it as a dialogue. Involve your adult child, listen to their perspective, and work together. Taking time to listen and respond promotes effective communication and prevents misunderstandings or resentment.

Open conversations about expectations can significantly improve your relationship with your adult child. Discussing unacceptable behaviors, respecting boundaries while maintaining connection, prioritizing each other's well-being, and avoiding guilt is beneficial. When boundaries are disrespected, discuss creating space and outline the consequences. When initiating a boundary discussion, ask open-ended questions like, "What are your thoughts about infringing on my personal space?" instead of, "Why do you bluntly disrespect my personal space?" Focus on active listening, prioritizing understanding, and validating their feelings rather than jumping to give advice or solve their problems. Show respect for their perspective and acknowledge their point of view. Have follow-up conversations based on the seriousness and complexity of the boundary.

Revisiting Boundaries: It's Ongoing

When revisiting boundaries with your adult child, it's important to approach it as an ongoing process. Boundaries may need to be adjusted and renegotiated as your situation and relationship evolve. For instance, when your adult child gets married or has children, the dynamics, and boundaries change.

Recognize changes and adjust boundaries. Keep communication open with your adult child to address issues and conflicts. Regular discussions to talk about expectations, needs, and concerns maintain a healthy and satisfying relationship. Ongoing communication about boundaries leads to less conflict and greater satisfaction. Keep channels open for both parties to express their thoughts and feelings openly and honestly. This promotes understanding and allows necessary boundary adjustments to support the changing relationship dynamics.

It's an ongoing process that requires open communication, flexibility, and mutual understanding. You can ensure your boundaries serve the evolving needs of your relationship with your adult child by staying open to change.

Keeping the Lines Open: No Boundaries

You need to keep talking to continue discussing and maintaining boundaries. Discuss old boundaries and establish new ones to maintain a healthy relationship. Keep communication open, address conflicts, and adapt boundaries as needed for a stronger relationship.

Here are some questions and activities to apply the concepts from the chapter:

- Reflect on your current boundaries with your adult child. Are there areas where you feel the boundaries are too rigid or too loose? How do these boundaries impact your relationship?
- Consider conflicts in your relationship with your adult child due to boundaries. How can you approach these to promote understanding and resolution? Can you make compromises or adjustments to find balance?
- Create a list of your parenting boundaries and non-negotiables for your well-being. Communicate these to your adult child in an open and respectful manner.
- Write a letter to your adult child expressing your thoughts and feelings about the boundaries in your relationship. Be honest about your intentions and expectations and the importance of maintaining a healthy balance between support and independence.

These questions and activities encourage self-reflection and conversations with your adult children. They help apply the chapter's concepts and strengthen the relationship with your adult child.

Fostering healthy connections with your adult child can blossom through deep relationships with clear boundaries.

Part 3: Build Strong and Resilient Relationships

As your child becomes an adult, you know your relationship will change. We will explore cultivating strong and lasting relationships with your adult children. We'll go beyond family bonds and guide you through building flourishing connections. Imagine your relationship with your adult child as a vibrant garden, ready for nurturing and growth. Encourage their independence while staying connected, embracing mutual respect, and adapting to change. By spending quality time together and fostering deeper bonds, you can create roots that grow stronger with time, able to withstand any challenges that may arise.

Your family tree continues to grow with the addition of in-laws and grandchildren. We will discuss the joys and challenges of these roles, providing guidance on navigating blended families and building lasting bonds across generations. Together, we will explore how to shape a legacy of love that will endure for years to come.

Life can throw unexpected challenges, straining even the strongest connections. Strong relationships, like a well-tended garden, can withstand storms and recover. In this part, we will provide tools and resources for navigating estrangement, guiding you through reconciliation, and offering acceptance, even in difficult circumstances where outcomes may be elusive.

As your adult children grow older, there may come a time when they become the support system for their aging parents. By fostering a resilient relationship with your adult children now, you are preparing for the possibility that roles may eventually shift. This ensures that love and support flow both ways.

This roadmap through Part 3 aims to equip you with the knowledge and confidence to cultivate strong and resilient relationships. It will help you nurture the bond with your adult child to withstand and flourish amidst life's many changes.

Chapter 9: Cultivate Strong Bonds— Growing Deeper Connections

Imagine your relationship with your adult child as a vibrant garden. Like any cherished plant, it requires attentive care to flourish. Forget rigid structure; think winding paths, diverse blooms, and ever-evolving beauty. This chapter guides you through nurturing deeper roots and stronger branches—"The Bonding Garden," where your connection thrives, no matter life's unpredictable challenges.

Ongoing care and attention are important in parent adult-child relationships. Patience allows your adult child to navigate their journey, make mistakes, and learn. Understanding involves seeing things from their perspective and accepting their individuality. By practicing patience and understanding, you create a supportive atmosphere for both parties to grow. This fosters a relationship built on trust, compassion, and respect. Developing a strong bond with your adult child requires a commitment to growth and learning together.

Deepening connections with your adult child is highly rewarding. It creates emotional closeness, open sharing of thoughts and feelings, and a deeper level of support and understanding. This fosters trust and respect. Your consistent support and guidance make them rely on you, providing a sense of belonging and security. Moreover, it creates a lasting intergenerational legacy, passing down values and connections.

Building a strong bond in a parent adult-child relationship requires effort and commitment from both parties. Providing support, guidance, and love by listening and offering advice while respecting their autonomy is essential. The adult child should actively participate by being open and honest, showing respect for their parent's guidance, and finding common interests. Spending quality time together and maintaining regular communication is essential. By mutually committing to the relationship, a deep and lasting connection can be cultivated. Let's dive in.

Cultivating a Strong Bond

Building a strong relationship with your adult child requires balancing their independence and fostering a deep connection. Creating a safe space for open communication is significant. It allows your adult child to express their thoughts and concerns without fear of judgment. This environment promotes trust and strengthens the bond between you. By actively listening and offering support without judgment, you create a foundation of understanding and acceptance that nurtures a lifelong connection. Maintaining a strong relationship requires ongoing effort and commitment, but the rewards are worth it.

Embracing your adult child's individuality and giving them space to explore their interests, passions, and goals is crucial for a healthy parent adult-child relationship. It's essential to recognize that their journey may not align with yours and support them in pursuing their unique path. This approach shows acceptance, encouragement, and belief in their growth. Our role as parents shifts from direct guidance to a supportive presence, offering wisdom and insight when sought, and respecting their autonomy and decision-making. Allowing our adult children to carve their own paths fosters self-discovery, independence, and fulfillment. Ultimately, by embracing their individuality, we build a strong bond based on trust, respect, and unconditional love.

Active listening is crucial for bonding with your adult child. Show genuine interest by asking open-ended questions that encourage meaningful conversations. Truly listen and demonstrate attentiveness by engaging in active dialogue. Create a safe space for open communication to give them the opportunity to share their experiences and perspectives. This fosters understanding and strengthens your connection. The key is to be present, empathetic, and genuinely interested.

Practicing empathy and understanding is crucial, especially during challenging times. Put yourself in your adult child's shoes and try to see things from their perspective. This can foster compassion and strengthen your bond. It shows your adult child that you genuinely care about their feelings and validate their experiences. By approaching situations with an open mind and heart, you can create a space for honest communication and connect with your adult child.

Imagine your adult child accomplishing something they've been working hard to achieve. In that moment, there's no one they want cheering them on more than you and their own family. You have the power to reinforce their confidence and self-worth in ways they'll never forget. Celebrating their achievements, no matter how small, creates a positive and supportive environment, nurturing a bond built on love and encouragement.

Wondering how to be a superpower for your adult child? Here are five simple ideas to celebrate their successes and make them feel seen and appreciated:

1. Celebrating your adult child's accomplishments brings joy to parents. It's important to convey your pride by expressing excitement and genuine admiration that resonates with your adult child. Acknowledge their hard work, dedication, and talent. Using specific words and highlighting their achievements ensures they feel seen and appreciated. Celebrate their successes and let them know you're their biggest fan. Your pride and admiration will provide unwavering encouragement, strengthening the bond between you.

2. Planning a special celebration to honor your adult child's achievements is a great way to show your care. Consider their preferences and interests when planning an activity or outing. It could be a family dinner at their favorite restaurant, a weekend getaway to a place they've always wanted to visit, or a small gathering with loved ones who have played a significant role in their journey. The key is to create an atmosphere that honors their accomplishments and makes them feel special. By planning a celebration, you're not only showing your love and support, but also creating lasting memories.

3. When celebrating your adult child's achievements, giving a meaningful gift can make their day. Consider something that shows thought and reflects their passions and personalities, rather than just trinkets and gadgets. For example, if they love reading, find a rare edition of their favorite novel. If they appreciate art, a piece from a local artist might resonate with them. Choose a gift with sentimental value to show support and appreciation. It's important to demonstrate that you took the time to think about what they would love and appreciate—something that speaks to their individuality. This personal touch will make the gift more memorable and meaningful. The value or cost of the gift is not as

important as the sentiment behind it. Get creative with your gift-giving and observe their faces light up with joy and gratitude. It's the thought and effort that truly matter when celebrating your adult child's achievements.

4. Write a heartfelt note or letter expressing your pride and admiration for their recent accomplishments. Highlight specific details that impressed you the most and how their hard work has made a positive impact. This gesture will serve as a treasured keepsake, allowing them to revisit your love and support. Your words can strengthen the bond between you and create lasting memories. Let your emotions guide your pen and deepen your connection with your adult child.

5. The importance of celebrating your adult child's successes cannot go unnoticed. Their accomplishments, big or small, are sparks of happiness. Being their number-one supporter is satisfying. By sharing their achievements with friends and family and on social media, unless social media is a boundary that would disrespect their privacy, you amplify the celebration and show your support and belief in their potential. Let the world know how proud you are of your adult child because when they shine, we all shine brighter!

Respecting Differences and Embracing Change

Respect your adult child's individuality, listen with an open mind, and show acceptance. Embrace changes in the family dynamic with joy. Utilize any form of communication for regular connection. Flexibility and understanding pave the way for a stronger, more resilient connection.

Be open-minded and receptive to new ideas. By fostering understanding, acceptance, and empathy, you create a space for healthy conversations. Encouraging open-mindedness allows for meaningful exchanges, while cultivating empathy helps you connect with your adult child's experiences and emotions. This approach will foster acceptance, growth, and a lasting connection.

Let's toast to mutual respect and tolerance! When parents and adult children make an effort, we all have a better time together. It keeps life surprising, interesting, and our minds open. Remember, they don't want to be us, and we don't want to be them. As someone said, "Being an adult is when you accept your parents for who they are." It's nice! While we salute our adult children's independence and respect their freedom, they need to do the same for us! It's reciprocal, and a great exchange! By fostering respect, tolerance, open-mindedness, and empathy, we can cultivate a vibrant "Bonding Garden" where both generations thrive, appreciate their differences, and enjoy the journey. When we began the parenting journey decades ago, our desire was always to do our best. We embarked on this new path, not knowing what was ahead. Parents never wake up in the morning declaring, "Today I'm going to mess up my kids." That is simply not how the task of parenting is approached. Give yourself grace for what hasn't gone as expected, and move forward with that same sense of doing your best.

Quality Time: Creating Memories

Nurturing your relationship with your adult child by creating one-on-one moments is important. Whether it's grabbing coffee, going for a walk, planning a vacation, enjoying family dinners, or having heartfelt conversations, these moments deepen connections and understanding. You can feel the bond grow stronger as you share experiences and create lasting memories. Explore new hobbies or interests together, like taking a cooking class, going on a road trip, or attending a concert or art exhibit. These shared experiences nourish your bond and create lasting memories. Don't underestimate their power. They are the building blocks of a meaningful connection.

Staying connected with our adult children can be challenging, especially with distance. But I have ideas to bridge the gap and create special moments, even when we're apart.

One fun activity to do if you're close enough to gather is to have a Virtual Cook-Off. Here's how it works: everyone gets the same ingredient list and creates a recipe. You can set a day to gather and taste each other's creations. This activity sparks creativity and culinary adventure, creating lasting memories. The ingredient list can rotate between family members, giving everyone a chance to challenge their culinary skills!

Now, I understand that virtual gatherings may not always be possible. But fear not! There are other ways to stay connected across the miles. One idea is to use technology and play games together using apps like Words With Friends. This virtual Scrabble game allows you to connect, compete, and have fun at your own pace. It's a great way to engage in friendly competition and stay connected.

Another way to stay connected is through regular texting. A thoughtful text can let your adult child know they're in your thoughts. I like to send a text, sometimes with a graphic or meme, to let my adult sons know I'm thinking of them. My challenge lies in accepting that they're busy and may not be interested in an exchange. I will send it anyway, even if I do not get a response. It warms my heart and lets them know of the constancy of our relationship. There can be a conversation about it when we're together, but for me, the act of sending is the message. My husband's mantra is "Give the gift freely." This applies to many scenarios, whether an actual gift or a message of love or thoughtfulness. Don't determine its value based on the response or lack of response.

Watching the same show or movie can create shared laughter and bring you closer, even when you're miles apart. Choose a show or movie that you both enjoy, synchronize your viewing, and set aside time to discuss it afterward. It's a great way to bond over shared interests. Value every interaction, even the virtual ones. These gestures, like a nostalgic song or a photo of a beloved pet, maintain the connection.

Underestimating the power of simple gestures and expressions of love and appreciation is a mistake. Sending a handwritten note or a small gift, expressing gratitude for their presence, or sharing a favorite family recipe are meaningful ways to keep the connection alive.

Remember, the quality of time together matters most. Despite the distance, you can create meaningful moments and lasting memories to nurture your relationship and keep your bond strong. Pick an activity that resonates with you and your adult child, and stay connected, no matter the distance. Enjoy, cherish, and embrace the joy of a strong bond.

Lasting Bonds: Love, Trust, and Respect

I understand the desire to always be a part of your adult child's life. The relationships they choose may seem more important, but your role as a parent isn't insignificant. The key is to create an environment where your adult children not only need you but also choose to maintain a bond with you. They will always be connected to you, but it's crucial to recognize that they can decide the level of engagement. It's important to approach this with maturity, realism, and an understanding of your role in their lives. To build a strong bond with your adult child, the essentials are love, trust, and mutual respect. Without these, misunderstandings and conflicts can strain the relationship. For example, an adult child shares, "I'm having a tough time with my parents at the moment. My mother constantly belittles my parenting, cleaning, lifestyle choices, and spending. I'm grateful that mutual respect is important to others."

Love goes beyond words; it requires action. Showing love means letting our adult children make mistakes and learn. It also means supporting them during tough times. Trust is built over time, through consistent and reliable actions. Keeping promises and being a dependable source of support strengthens trust in our relationship with adult children.

How can we implement this in our own lives? One way is by being present and showing up for our adult children when they need us. Whether it's offering a listening ear, providing words of encouragement, or lending a helping hand, these actions demonstrate our love and support. Another way is by respecting their autonomy and individuality. This means allowing them to make their own decisions, even if we disagree, and trusting in their ability to navigate their own lives.

Be mindful of consistency and reliability. Our adult children need to know they can count on us, in good and bad times. By keeping our promises and showing up consistently, we build trust and a strong bond.

Ultimately, the combination of love, support, respect, and reliability builds a deep connection with our adult children. By demonstrating our love through our actions, we create a nurturing environment for our relationships to flourish. Let's put our love into action and build a lasting bond with our adult children.

Keeping the Lines Open: Path to Deeper Understanding

Communication is essential for a thriving "Bonding Garden." Just as tending to plants requires regular attention, nurturing your relationship also requires open communication. I encourage heartfelt conversations with your children. Share your first heartbreak or weird quirk. Have awkward, unfiltered conversations. Be vulnerable. Show them you're not always strong, but you're still standing, and they can too. These conversations will strengthen your bond. Immerse yourself in knowing your adult children. They have changed and may have wisdom you lack. Love, trust, and mutual respect come from openness and vulnerability. Reflect on the following:

- Recall a significant challenge or disappointment. What did you learn? How did you overcome it? Create a "Life Stories Jar" where you and your adult child write and share a story from your past, drawing one randomly at each conversation.
- Do I create a safe space for my adult child to share their feelings and opinions?
- Am I doing my best to understand their perspective?
- Do I communicate my needs and boundaries clearly and respectfully to my adult child?
- Do we have regular, meaningful conversations that aren't about solving problems?

Reflect on these questions and practice mindful communication to strengthen your relationship foundation. Cultivate love, trust, and respect to enhance your connection and build a lifelong bond. The bond between parents and adult children is ongoing. Building it takes time and patience and is rewarding.

With these tools, you're prepared to navigate the expanded family roles in Chapter 10: In-Laws and Grandparenting. Get ready to discover the joys and challenges of this next chapter in your journey!

Chapter 10: In-Law and Grandparents—Navigating New Territories

Welcome to a thrilling twist in your family narrative! As your children grow, their journeys expand to include partners and little ones, inviting you into new roles as an in-law and grandparent. This role can be exciting, but it's normal to feel clueless and need to find your balance again. Navigating these new situations can be overwhelming, but this chapter provides guidance on how to navigate your evolving roles for a harmonious extended family experience.

Watching your children become parents is magical, and it ushers in a new chapter. Navigating your role as a grandparent can be exciting, yet tricky. Balancing support with respect for their parenting style, understanding boundaries, and offering wisdom without imposing demands are crucial for fostering positive connections.

Striking a Balance: Your New In-Law Identity

Starting new families and getting to know your extended family can be challenging but not impossible. Getting along with your in-laws can be hard work. As you become an in-law, it's essential to recognize the shift from being solely your adult child's parent to now being part of a larger family dynamic. It's important to approach this relationship with an open mind and a willingness to learn and understand. Building a positive relationship with your in-laws takes time and effort from both sides. Be open to getting to know them and their perspectives. For me, learning the new relationship of being a daughter-in-law became about respect. My new in-laws loved and raised the person I was choosing to marry. It was in everyone's best interest to keep this in mind and respect their role in our new family dynamic.

Dealing with a new in-law can be tricky. Their background can shape them to be kind or tough. My interaction with them sets a tone and builds a future. An ex-daughter-in-law was separated from my son, and I expressed my sadness but wished them both happiness. I never want to encourage divorce, but sometimes it's the best outcome. Acceptance in these moments is crucial. They got back together for a time, and if I had 'burned that bridge' by being judgmental or harsh, it could have made things more difficult. I don't have to live with my in-laws. Our sons and daughters have chosen who to live with, and my goal is for them to be happy. It's not about me. I am part of the family.

Your relationship with your adult child's spouse is crucial for a positive extended family dynamic. Being accepting, respectful, and non-judgmental can contribute to a harmonious relationship. This creates a supportive network for your adult child and their spouse. Giving them space while remaining supportive and having open and constructive conversations can build a strong bond within your extended family.

How do I avoid common mistakes like taking sides or offering unsolicited advice? When offering advice or opinions, I should ensure that my adult child and their spouse have invited me into the conversation. I should focus on being a supportive listener, offering guidance when asked, and staying neutral in conflicts.

Mutual respect and open communication are key to building a strong extended family. Communicate your expectations and respect your adult child's boundaries. Embrace and adapt to changes, staying open-minded and understanding.

Navigate your new role as an in-law and foster harmonious relationships within your extended family with open communication, respect, and support. Create a strong family unit by building genuine connections and maintaining healthy boundaries. Embrace the opportunity to learn and grow. Contribute to an extended family network that is supportive and harmonious by fostering positive, respectful, and open relationships with your in-laws.

The Joys and Challenges of Grandparenthood

Becoming a grandparent is significantly different from being a parent. The beauty lies in witnessing your adult child become a parent and their love for their children. Observing glimpses of my adult child's development is captivating. Their individual personalities, a combination of familiar and unique traits, fill me with awe. You have the opportunity to form fresh and meaningful connections with your grandchildren and witness their growth. Furthermore, as you witness your adult child step into the role of a parent, you have the privilege of being a mentor to this new generation, guiding and supporting them. Navigating the evolving dynamics between all the individuals involved is constantly changing, creating a mix of joy and challenge. I approach these relationships with love and acknowledge that my time with them is limited. What impact do I want these moments to have on them, whether it's my son or daughter, their partners, or my grandchild? I strive to emanate care, patience, understanding, and optimism.

When your adult child recognizes the connection between their child and you, it brings them great joy and satisfaction. They feel validated in their own parenting when they see their child surrounded by additional sources of love, support, and wisdom. As a grandparent actively involved in their grandchildren's lives, you become an extended support system for your adult child. This support can be especially valuable if your adult child is facing parenting challenges or going through their own life changes. The bond between you and your grandchildren can give your adult child some much-needed time to recharge, focus on their own needs, or attend to other responsibilities. It creates a sense of balance and helps prevent feelings of being overwhelmed or isolated. It can also provide reassurance that they have an ally in you, someone who understands the joys and difficulties of raising children. By being a trusted confidante, a loving presence, and a source of guidance, you become an essential pillar in your family's legacy, ensuring that love and understanding continue to thrive for generations to come.

Not all people become grandparents in the same way. Research shows that nearly 95% of older adults with adult children become grandparents. Some become grandparents through their adult children's marriage to partners with children, while others may adopt the role of children in their extended family or community. Becoming a grandparent opens new opportunities for connection, mentoring, and passing on values and family identity (Brotherson et al., 2020).

The Joys of Grandparenthood

Many find grandparenting meaningful. Grandparents impart identity, unconditional love, support, wisdom, and encouragement to their grandchildren. They offer hope, stability, and security, embody positive values, serve as mentors and teachers, nurture their well-being, and act as role models and play companions. They shape their lives and create lasting memories.

Being a grandparent is an extremely rewarding experience. It provides an opportunity to develop a special bond with your grandchildren and witness their growth. This bond is nurtured through regular contact, whether in person or through technology, shared values, and strong family connections. Sharing stories, providing support, and consistently showing love build trust and closeness. The happiness of being a grandparent is mutual. Simply being present and participating in their activities brings immense joy. When they express a desire to spend time with you, introduce you to their friends, or share their interests, it fills your heart with happiness and gratitude.

Becoming grandparents shifts our values and perspectives. Research shows that having a grandchild changes our values, making life feel more meaningful and satisfying in a new way (Maijala et al., 2012). We learn to accept aging and appreciate the younger generation more. There is this "extended ease" where the relationship is characterized by affection and care, but with a different dynamic than the parent-child relationship. Grandparents experience a sweeter and easier love without the same level of responsibilities as parenting. However, it's often more relaxed and joyful than parenthood. Building a relationship with a young human may seem intimidating, but being a grandparent brings ease and fulfillment from embracing the bond. Each grandparent has a unique relationship with each grandchild, making the experience special. The grandparent-grandchild relationship can be celebrated and cherished for its joyful and supportive qualities, allowing for a different kind of love and connection. It's important to keep in mind, though, that as grandchildren grow, it's important to respect their independence while providing guidance when needed. Embracing change and adapting to evolving family dynamics allows the bond to develop naturally, preserving this cherished connection.

Becoming a grandparent also brings significant changes to your daily life, such as grocery shopping, cooking, and planning activities with grandchildren during holidays. It is common for grandparents to spend holidays with their grandchildren, either by having them visit or staying for multiple days, particularly if they live far away.

By nurturing this special relationship, grandparents and grandchildren create a source of love, support, and happiness. This enriches their lives and strengthens the family's legacy, ensuring that the tapestry woven with love and understanding continues to grow for generations to come. Embracing the role of a grandparent brings acceptance and renewed energy for older parents. Despite aging, grandparents are willing to try new experiences with their grandchildren. Creating pleasant memories and adventures becomes a priority for both.

Grandparenthood is positive, but it has challenges that should be recognized and addressed.

The Challenges of Grandparenthood

Maintaining relationships within extended families can be challenging. It requires communication, openness, and flexibility. Challenges can arise when becoming a grandparent due to differences in child-rearing principles, excessive intervention, a lack of openness, or grandparents feeling taken for granted. There are also other challenges like distance, lack of time, and conflicts that can damage these threads that connect generations. However, approaching these challenges with maturity and understanding can help navigate them more positively. Both grandparents and adult children need to work on understanding, flexibility, and respecting each other's lives to avoid tension and promote well-being.

Divorce rates have increased, posing challenges for today's grandparents. It affects all family relationships, including the bond between grandparents and grandchildren. Single parents may need more support from their parents. Relationships with adult children's spouses may be problematic, affecting the grandparent-grandchild relationship. Differences among grandchildren can vary based on personalities and social development (Maijala et al., 2012).

Finding quality time with grandchildren can be challenging, especially for working grandparents with limited availability on weekends and holidays. Retired grandparents may have more time, but they also have commitments, friends, and hobbies to balance. Waiting for visits and missing time with grandchildren can be emotionally challenging. Of course, geographic distance is a big factor in the grandparenting relationship. There is nothing better than face-to-face, but that isn't always possible.

Grandparents face hurdles in coping with the demands of grandparenthood, influenced by their physical health, time with grandchildren, and balancing work. It's important for them to recognize their limitations and take care of themselves while being present for their grandchildren by managing energy levels, setting boundaries, and finding support.

As our grandchildren grow, they become more independent and develop their own interests and priorities. It's important for us, as grandparents, to understand and respect that they may have less time for us as they navigate school, friends, and activities. We may notice that the activities we used to enjoy together may change as we pursue new hobbies and experiences. It might feel disappointing, but it's the natural evolution of this relationship. Expecting such change makes it easier to navigate.

Grandparents have their own ideas about raising their grandchildren, but it's important to recognize that the parents have the primary responsibility. Grandparents can teach important skills, but they should respect the parents' rules and guidelines. It's necessary for the rules and boundaries to align, and adult children should be aware of which to follow.

Embracing the role of a grandparent can be challenging, as they may face unfamiliar territory with school subjects, technology, and new trends, as well as taking care of grandchildren and housework.

As grandchildren grow, grandparents have the heartfelt desire to understand their responsibilities and become role models. Grandchildren have a natural curiosity and may ask countless questions, challenging the grandparents' knowledge. My grandchildren enjoy stories about our younger years as well as stories about their parents. It's fun to recount these with them.

Types of Grandparenthood

A grandparent can deny, compensate, withdraw, or enjoy grandparenthood. A denying grandparent may struggle to accept aging and the continuity of life, find it difficult to embrace the new generation, and may not be ready for the joys and responsibilities of grandparenthood. Some claim they are too young to be grandparents, so they adopt titles other than Grandma and/or Grandpa.

A compensating grandparent is in good physical shape, accepting of their aging process, and has a thriving social network. However, they may not feel ready to fully embrace the role of being a grandparent, prioritize their work and personal activities, and not have the capacity or desire to be involved in their grandchild's life. Withdrawing from grandparenthood can happen when the grandparent is willing but lacks resources, such as physical condition, coping skills, or social relationships. Issues with adult children, in-laws, or divorce can also affect grandparenthood.

As a grandparent, you're ready to embrace the changes and challenges of this stage of life. You understand the importance of aging and generational continuity and find fulfillment in spending quality time with your grandchildren.

Navigating the Extended Family

Becoming a grandparent can involve navigating complex dynamics within the extended family. Adding a new member can create tension. Navigating relationships with your adult child's in-laws can be challenging. It's important to be respectful, open-minded, and build positive relationships with them by finding common interests, inviting them to family events, and getting to know them better.

Managing extended family relationships can be a challenge. It's important to balance time with your grandchild and respect other family members' wishes. Open communication about expectations and finding ways to share time can help.

Respect family members' wishes; avoid taking sides or getting involved in conflicts. Focus on building a positive relationship with your grandchild and supporting their emotional well-being.

Managing Expectations

Becoming a grandparent is an exciting role filled with joys and potential obstacles. It's important to recognize that your role is different from that of a parent and to respect the wishes and parenting style of your adult child. This includes managing expectations, understanding that your child and their partner may have other priorities, and being open and flexible. Every grandparent-grandchild relationship is unique, and your grandchild may have different interests and personalities. Embrace open-mindedness and patience and build a positive relationship with your grandchild. Sometimes, the easiest way to let distant grandchildren know you are thinking about them is to send a video or picture of a gift they gave you. This lets them know you appreciate it and they are close at heart.

Managing your expectations as a new grandparent involves accepting that your grandchild will grow and change. They will develop their own interests, move away, or experience other transitions. It's important to be flexible and adaptable. Being a grandparent is a journey of learning, growth, and understanding. Celebrate your role, honor their individuality, and create lasting memories through communication, respect, and love. By fostering a strong relationship, you can contribute to their well-being and create a legacy of love within your family.

Psychologist Erik Erikson suggested that the most significant task of adulthood is giving ourselves to the next generation. It's worth considering what we have to offer and hope to give to our grandchildren (Cherry, 2023).

Supporting Your Adult Children's Parenting

Being a grandparent means offering support, wisdom, and a listening ear, not trying to direct your adult child's parenting style. Understand the difference between guidance and direction. Adjusting to a more supportive role can be tricky. Respect your adult child's decisions, even when you disagree. Building a strong bond with your grandchildren takes time and effort. Find ways to connect that respect your adult child's boundaries, like playing games, reading stories, or enjoying quality time together. There may be times when you work on something in the same space without conversation. It might seem challenging, but it can build a connection as strong as chatting. I love coloring with my grandchildren, and it's common not to talk. Admiring each other's creations is satisfying.

Embrace bonding with your grandchildren and experiencing parenthood from a new perspective. Your role complements, not replaces, your adult child's parenting. This journey requires collaboration, a gift, and a challenge. Your presence and consistency impact those young lives. Openness and appreciation for each other's roles will unlock more joy for everyone.

Keeping the Lines Open: Fostering Harmony

Navigating your grandparent role isn't about scripted interactions or rigid rules. It's about genuine connection, and communication is essential. Open and honest conversations are vital for harmony. Here are some key takeaways:

Listen to your adult children, their partners, and grandchildren with an open mind and heart. Seek to understand their perspectives and show genuine interest. Express your thoughts and feelings clearly and respectfully, even when disagreeing. Avoid judgment, address conflicts constructively, and seek common ground and solutions.

Show love and support through actions, not just words. Spend quality time, offer help without intruding, and create lasting memories. Our family has adopted the habit of providing a one-hour notice before visiting our one son to show respect for his household. Our agreement is that we do not get offended if the time isn't right. It has become a running joke, especially if I provide less than one hour's notice, taken humorously and respectfully.

Reflecting on your experiences and ideas can enhance your role as a grandparent. Consider the following:

- Did you have a close relationship with your grandparents?
- How did you feel when your first grandchild was born?

- Do you picture yourself as the emotional leader of your family?
- What can you uniquely teach your grandchild?
- What would you like to pass on to your grandchild?
- How do you respectfully communicate your disagreement with your adult child's parenting decisions while respecting their role as a parent?
- Think of a time you felt unheard or misunderstood by your family. How can you actively listen and ensure clear communication as an in-law or grandparent?
- Did your parents or in-laws offer helpful support during your early parenting years? Or did their involvement make things more challenging?
- Discuss with your adult child and their partner how to contribute to open and regular family communication. What ground rules or practices can you establish to foster healthy communication?

We choose actions to build lasting memories with our grandchildren.

Chapter 11: Estrangement

Estrangement is a heavy word, carrying the burden of silence and shattered connections. This painful disconnection can feel overwhelming for parents who long for connection with their adult children. The parent adult-child relationship can endure hardships, but estrangement can leave it frayed. This emotional wound reveals vulnerability, fractured trust, and unfulfilled dreams from the parents' perspective. As expectations and dreams unravel alongside estrangement, parents face a stark reality far from their hopes. In this disappointment, guilt and self-doubt add vulnerability. Yet, even across this distance, hope flickers.

Estrangement is painful, regardless of the relationship. Being estranged from a son or daughter you've birthed, raised, loved, and nurtured can be an indescribable loss. Estrangement is unique to each relationship, even if they have been under the same roof for years. Accepting this unwelcome circumstance is a great challenge. Parents want to know their children, to love them, and to connect with them. It's important to keep in mind that each party involved experiences estrangement differently, and what one person may perceive as estrangement may not be the same for the other. Relationships change, and what may feel distant could unexpectedly shift and regain connection. While this is not always the case, it's healthy to maintain open channels and be flexible without extreme emotional outbursts.

Relationships with adult children can become strained and lead to estrangement, a painful reality for some families. This highlights the deep wound of parental rejection, as a once vibrant connection becomes strained. Trust and security thin with each unanswered call or unopened message, casting uncertainty. Parents fear recurring estrangement. Estrangement goes beyond physical separation to emotional disconnect. This strain unravels the family unit. Shared memories become inaccessible, leaving a hole where laughter and love reside. The shared identity crumbles, replaced by isolation and a yearning for connection. There are a larger number of estranged relationships than we might think (Gilligan et al., 2015). Estrangement occurs due to prolonged tension, with one person deciding to cut off communication for various reasons. It's important to acknowledge that reconciliation may not happen, despite our best efforts. This acceptance can be heartbreaking, devastating, and life-changing. It's important to remember that healing and growth can occur without reconciliation. Focus on finding peace within yourself and nurturing other supportive relationships. Prioritize your well-being and allow yourself space to heal and move forward, even if it means letting go of the hope for reconciliation.

Understanding Estrangement: An Unraveled Bond

Sometimes, when I think about family, I imagine it as a tapestry— a creation made of tightly woven threads creating a beautiful image representing shared experiences and love. But what happens when a thread frays and becomes loose, threatening to unravel the fabric? This is where estrangement comes in. It's not just physical separation; it's the emotional disconnect that creates problems in our families. Surprisingly, more parents than we realize face this painful reality, each with unique stories filled with different causes and challenges. It could be divorce, differences in values, or unresolved childhood issues. Unfortunately, there's no universal solution. However, experts from the Stanford

Medicine WellMD Center suggest that the first step toward repairing the broken connection is to acknowledge the pain, for both parents and their adult children. From there, the approach can vary—open communication, therapy, or mediation, depending on the specific threads that need mending. The key is to have genuine empathy, open communication, and a willingness to acknowledge the hurt on both sides. It's not an easy process, and there may be scars left behind. But by acknowledging the vulnerability and working towards understanding, we can create a more resilient tapestry, interwoven with threads of compassion and hope.

Estrangement from your child is one of the most painful experiences. Whether you crossed a boundary, or your adult child did, the pain is the same. Reasons for estrangement can further include significant life events like marriage or childbirth. These causes can be categorized into three main areas.

The first cause is related to personality changes as children grow older, becoming incompatible with our own. Factors like mental illness or traumatic brain injuries can also drastically alter a person's personality. Differences in values, sexual orientation, or religious beliefs can create a rift between parents and adult children.

The second cause is negative behavior stemming from a history of abuse, neglect, or distant parenting. Harsh parenting styles characterized by manipulation and control can lead to resentment. When conflicts persist and are left unresolved for years, it often leads to one person ending the relationship.

The third cause is external issues. For example, physical distance can erode the connection between family members. When one person feels they're investing more than the other, they may withdraw. In some cases, a son or daughter may be in a relationship with an abusive partner who isolates them from their family. It's important to recognize the signs and intervene, if possible, to protect your adult child. It is always important though to remember you only see from one side of the relationship, so approaching with grace can be a critical difference.

Every family dynamic is unique, so there's no universal solution for resolving estrangement. Strategies based on your knowledge of your adult child and their preferences can help. Open and honest communication is key to addressing issues and repairing the relationship. Find an appropriate time and place to talk. Actively listen to their perspective and take ownership of any mistakes. Therapy can address underlying issues and work towards healing. If professional help isn't feasible, enlist the support of a neutral friend or family member to mediate. Each situation requires a tailored approach that may take time and persistence.

You know your child and their preferred approach to reconciliation. Some adult children can handle confrontation, while others need space and time to heal.

The First Step: Reaching Out

Initiating contact is sensitive. Rushing in can widen the gap. Express your desire to reconnect without blame or demands. Swallow your pride and extend the proverbial olive branch for reconciliation. Even if you don't believe you were solely at fault, offering an apology can open the door to conversation. Taking these steps with a mature and realistic attitude will foster a relatable atmosphere, facilitating a friendly dialogue with your child.

Initiating contact after estrangement is challenging. It requires a mature approach that considers both parties. Instead of pushing for immediate action, offer an open door without blame or demands. Everyone heals at their own pace, and the timeline for reconciliation may differ. It could take weeks, months, or years. The key is to remain compassionate, understanding, and patient. Respect the other person's boundaries and emotions. Healing a relationship takes time, effort, and empathetic communication.

Apologies are powerful for initiating meaningful conversations and fostering reconciliation. They show a willingness to let go of pride and extend an olive branch to your child. It's not easy to accept responsibility for conflict and estrangement, even if it's not entirely our fault. Yet, being able to acknowledge our mistakes and sincerely apologize shows our adult child that we recognize our humanity and fallibility. Making mistakes is unavoidable; what matters is how we handle them and rectify the situation. Some mistakes are easier to fix than others, especially when they are deeply rooted in our personality traits. Acknowledging these negative traits is difficult but essential. It allows us to recognize the influence they may have on our judgment during challenging times and take the necessary steps to address them.

As a mature and realistic person, it's important to reflect on our own actions and be open to personal growth. We should strive to communicate in a relatable and friendly manner, creating an atmosphere of empathy and understanding. Accepting our flaws and making amends can pave the way for a healthier, more connected relationship with our adult child.

Sometimes, we find ourselves making the same mistakes that caused the initial conflict with our adult child. It's important to recognize these patterns and make a conscious effort to start over. Take a moment to choose your words carefully and reframe what you want to say. If your previous words were rude, shift to a polite and considerate tone. If impatience gets the best of you, take a deep breath and count to ten before responding. By recognizing and correcting these mistakes earlier, you can show your adult child that it wasn't your intention to hurt them.

Sometimes words can only convey so much, and they fall short of capturing the depth of our feelings. In these cases, initiating physical contact can be powerful. If your child is open to it, offer a hug or simply touch their hand. This physical connection can help bring back feelings of closeness and strengthen the bond between you.

Another helpful strategy is to set a date and do something enjoyable together. By engaging in a shared activity, you can reestablish a connection that might have been strained during the conflict resolution process. This activity not only fills the silence that may occur after resolving a conflict but also creates new pleasant memories for both of you.

Parents grapple with deep loneliness, rejection, and societal judgment, while their adult children face their own vulnerabilities and emotional complexities that contribute to the estrangement. Recognizing and acknowledging the vulnerability on all sides is crucial for healing and understanding. Encouraging open communication and considering the perspectives of both parents and children is important.

Grandparenthood, a role often seen as a time of love and affection, also involves a layer of vulnerability. While the happiness of connecting with new family members is undeniable, embracing this vulnerability allows for deeper, more meaningful relationships. The transition to grandparenthood brings waves of emotions. Letting go of parental control, navigating potential conflicts, and forming connections with in-laws and grandchildren all require vulnerability. Stepping outside our comfort zones, expressing emotions openly, and respecting boundaries build trust and understanding. This dynamic remains the same even in the face of estrangement.

Building Trust: A Step-by-Step Journey

Rebuilding trust demands unwavering patience and consistent action. It's crucial to respect your adult child's boundaries, even when challenging, as actions have a more significant impact than mere words. Demonstrate genuine positive change through your behavior, confronting past issues directly, and recognizing the sacrifices your adult child has made. These actions will serve as the foundation upon which trust can be rebuilt. This journey takes time, particularly after enduring deep fractures. Embody patience in every action you take, ensuring that your words align seamlessly with your behavior. Aim to be a reliable and trustworthy person whose actions clearly show their commitment to rebuilding the relationship.

Rebuilding trust requires a visible change in your actions. Your words need to align with your consistent behavior, as this gives credibility to both words and actions. To rebuild a relationship with your adult child, be willing to let go of the behaviors and attitudes that caused tension in the first place. For example, if you have a tendency to react defensively and shout when confronted, try to lower your voice, listen attentively before responding, and show that you are actively making an effort to change. By doing so, you are demonstrating your commitment to rebuilding the relationship and giving your adult child the assurance that genuine change is taking place.

As you progress, it is important to have open and honest discussions about the new expectations that both you and your adult child have. This is a chance to reassess and redefine boundaries that may have been previously established, as well as find common ground in the newly forged chapter of this relationship. While this phase may initially feel challenging and complex, it's important to take your time and continue putting in the effort. Approach this stage of your life with caution, understanding that engaging in negative behaviors could jeopardize all the progress you have worked so hard to achieve.

Be mature and realistic in your approach, maintaining a personal connection by fostering relatable and friendly interactions. Providing informative insights can help create a supportive and understanding environment as you rebuild trust and connection with your child. Every step you take is an opportunity to strengthen the bond and build a more resilient relationship.

Keeping the Lines Open: Whispers Across the Bridge

Communication, the essential thread woven throughout this chapter and this book, remains paramount. Estrangement often results from a breakdown in communication and demands your own preferences. While some bridges may never fully rebuild, whispering across the bridge, however small, allows for the possibility of future connection. Now that you have journeyed through this chapter, ponder these questions:

- Do you have any personal experiences with estrangement in your family or close relationships?
- Can you imagine situations in your family where reconciliation after estrangement might not be possible or desirable?
- Consider writing a journal about personal stories, analyzing conflicts, or reflecting on your hopes and fears for the future.
- Do you find processing and expressing emotions challenging? Is it difficult to put your experiences of estrangement into words? Explore the theme of estrangement through artwork, music, poetry, or any other creative medium that resonates with you.

Estrangement is a complex issue with no easy answers. There is no single right way to navigate it, and the process will be unique to you and your family. Focus on self-care and personal growth, regardless of the outcome of the situation. You are worthy of love and happiness, regardless of the choices of others. With understanding, empathy, and unwavering hope for connection, even seemingly insurmountable bridges can be crossed, step by tentative step.

Chapter 12: The Murky Crystal Ball—Weathering Relationships

Life rarely unfolds along predictable paths. What if the roles reverse, and you find yourself needing support from your adult child, be it financial or emotional? Navigating this role reversal can be challenging and humbling. This chapter explores how to navigate this delicate situation, ensuring your relationship remains resilient and supportive through life's unpredictable stormy weather.

When the Tables Turn: Navigating Financial Support

Proactive Financial Planning

While our main objective as parents is to raise independent adult children, life is not always straightforward. As we grow older, the possibility of needing financial support from our adult children becomes a possible reality. None of us want to rely on our adult children for financial assistance or feel like a burden. One important piece of advice when it comes to financial planning is to plan ahead. While we cannot predict the future, it is possible to carefully strategize for the years to come. Have conversations with your adult children. Consider discussing topics such as alternative living arrangements if living alone at home becomes impractical, the existence of a will, and the allocation of funds for potential care expenses. Although these discussions may be sensitive, open and honest dialogue is essential. Looking at options like long-term care insurance can help should increased care needs become necessary.

It's obvious: save now, enjoy later, and reduce bills. By setting aside even small amounts regularly, you can create a surprisingly large nest egg by the time you reach retirement. However, there are many adult children who willingly live at home to help out their parents (Singletary, 2023). As parents, it becomes crucial for us to respect their financial boundaries and communicate openly about our financial situation. Proactive financial planning can greatly reduce the burden on both ourselves and our adult children. By keeping them informed about our finances, we can work together to put contingency plans in place. Having these plans not only eases the potential stress of the situation but also mentally and emotionally prepares both parties for the possible change. Therefore, it's important to maintain open communication when discussing our financial needs and expectations with our adult children.

Having a contingency plan reduces panic and allows for more informed decision-making. When individuals expect and prepare for potential events, they can create a clear action plan that promotes a sense of progress and unity with their adult children. Additionally, a contingency plan can help prioritize pressing financial matters, such as the risk of losing one's home. In this case, individuals may choose to seek assistance from their adult children for mortgage payments or consider downsizing to a more affordable home. Other options, such as moving to a nursing home or requesting a loan from adult children for medical bills, insurance, or credit card debt, can also be explored. The most suitable course of action will depend on the specific circumstances and desired outcomes.

One way to reduce the burden on your adult children while showcasing your autonomy and commitment to being responsible is by taking measures in your financial planning, including retirement and potential healthcare needs.

Investing in Expertise

Financial advisors are not just for the wealthy. Their expertise is invaluable in creating financial projections, exploring various scenarios, and ensuring your retirement and healthcare needs are met. Consider it an investment in your future security and a way to minimize the potential burden on your adult children. A financial advisor can provide assistance in a wide range of areas. While this brief description doesn't cover everything, it can give you a sense of the holistic financial advice they can offer.

A financial advisor can assist you in estate planning, which involves ensuring that your assets are distributed according to your wishes while minimizing inheritance taxes for your adult children. They can also help you create powers of attorney and healthcare directives, which allow trusted individuals to make financial and medical decisions on your behalf if you become unable to do so. Additionally, if you have grandchildren, a financial advisor can help you develop strategies to save for their future education needs and navigate the financial implications of different funding options and financial aid. Furthermore, they can guide you in transferring wealth to your adult children while also preserving your own financial security and minimizing tax implications. Lastly, they can optimize your retirement savings and investments to ensure that you have a comfortable and secure retirement.

Another important area where they can offer guidance is assessing potential sources of income in retirement, such as Social Security, pensions, and investment income. Also within their expertise is healthcare planning for retirees, including understanding Medicare and long-term care insurance options. They can analyze your insurance needs, such as life insurance and disability insurance, and develop strategies to protect your assets from risks like market downturns or unexpected healthcare expenses. We recently had a local fiduciary evaluate our investments and insurance. It is definitely a worthwhile investment. Some adjustments and surprises surfaced, which made the process even more valuable to us.

Another area where a financial advisor can provide valuable guidance is minimizing tax burdens throughout your life and in retirement. They can stay up-to-date with changing tax laws and explain how these laws impact your financial situation.

Financial advisors can assist with tasks like handling monthly bills, maintaining balanced budgets, overseeing investments and financial transactions, providing advice on investment security, negotiating with creditors on your behalf, and even helping with real estate investments. Their expertise can help you navigate these financial decisions with confidence.

Navigating Reverse Parenting: Valuing Non-Financial Support

Sometimes in life, the roles we once knew can change, and our adult children find themselves caring for us in our advancing years. Assuming the responsibility of providing care for aging parents can be difficult. They want nothing more than to be caring and supportive and to see you happy. However, it's important to remember that they are humans, too, and caregiving can be tiring and emotionally draining at times. The delicate balance between being an adult child and acting as a parent can blur the lines of traditional roles within the family and create tension if not navigated carefully.

In these moments of reverse parenting, additional complexity can enter relationships. This change can also lead to physical or emotional distance. This requires clear communication and setting expectations to avoid misunderstandings and reduce distance as much as possible. By openly discussing roles and responsibilities from the beginning, we establish a foundation for a smoother journey ahead. It's crucial to show appreciation for their efforts and acknowledge the sacrifices they make. Support your adult child as they transition into this role. Offer reminders to seek help when needed, as they may feel unsure or unprepared for taking up parenting responsibilities. Reassure them that their efforts are always sufficient. Embrace a grateful and humble attitude, expressing sincere love and appreciation for every gesture and act of kindness.

We all need emotional support from our loved ones. Companionship and quality time make a difference in our lives. Sometimes, we crave simply spending time together without discussing finances or worries. It's about enjoying shared activities, pursuing hobbies, or relishing each other's company. In these moments, we have someone to talk to who empathetically listens and validates our joys, frustrations, and concerns without judgment. We long for reassurance and encouragement—someone who supports our decisions and life choices. And let's not forget the importance of celebrating achievements and milestones.

Having practical support from your adult children is helpful. It can come in the form of an extra pair of hands, such as to help with errands and chores. They can lend a hand with grocery shopping, laundry, home repairs, or yard work. Having someone available for transportation and mobility can be incredibly valuable, especially if your mobility is limited. Technological challenges can also be overwhelming in today's digital age. That's where your adult children can step in, whether it's navigating a smartphone or setting up new devices. And let's not forget pet care or house-sitting when you're away or need some support. Having your adult children help with these responsibilities can provide peace of mind.

Social support is vital for well-being. Adult children can also be crucial in this aspect, connecting you with friends and family, encouraging socialization, participation in activities, and maintaining connections with loved ones. They can even introduce you to new social circles or activities, helping you find new hobbies, interests, or groups to join. This is particularly beneficial if you have social anxiety or a lack of belonging in social situations.

Mutual respect and gratitude serve as the basis for a cohesive and fulfilling family dynamic during this phase of life. They are important in navigating reverse parenting dynamics and valuing non-monetary support. Respecting your adult children's autonomy while accepting their help is important because they are offering assistance out of love. So, it's important not to make them feel obligated. Remember the boundaries we discussed earlier and put them into practice. Give your adult child the opportunity to know what specific areas would be most helpful. The love, companionship, and practical help from your adult children and other family members are priceless treasures. Don't hesitate to ask for the type of support you need, appreciate it with all your heart, and express your gratitude openly.

Exploring Deeper Emotional Support Needs

Emotional support goes beyond specific tasks and encompasses deeper dimensions that can significantly impact your well-being. Here are some additional aspects to consider:

Knowing that your adult children appreciate and cherish you unconditionally, regardless of life's circumstances or changes, is incredibly meaningful and creates a profound sense of belonging. The memories and experiences you share with them strengthen the bond you have, establishing a deep sense of connection within your family. When they value your opinions and feelings, it cultivates a rich sense of respect. This foundation of love, understanding, and communication is what sustains and nurtures your relationship, allowing it to withstand the challenges that life brings.

Having a judgment-free space where you can openly express your emotions and be confident is incredibly comforting and emotionally secure. You can confide in your adult children, knowing that they will provide unwavering support and understanding. Believing in your capabilities and receiving support for your goals and aspirations from your adult children boosts your confidence and motivation. Their words of encouragement and positive reinforcement fuel your sense of purpose and drive. The moments of joy and lightheartedness shared with your children create lasting memories that uplift your spirits and contribute to your overall well-being.

It's essential to recognize that our experiences and perspectives hold value, regardless of our age or circumstances. Finding meaning and purpose in life becomes even more important as you grow older.

Keeping the Lines Open: Communication Is the Bridge

Remember the vibrant garden metaphor? Open and honest communication is the water that nourishes it. Throughout this chapter, we've emphasized the importance of clear communication regarding financial needs and deeper emotional support. This extends to all aspects of your relationship with your adult children. Regularly discuss hopes, concerns, and changes in your lives, fostering mutual understanding and empathy. To help you gauge and manage this, you are welcome to ponder and reflect on the following:

- Have you prepared financially for your future needs? Do you have adequate savings, retirement plans, and healthcare coverage? Discuss this openly with your adult children.
- What kind of emotional support do you need and expect from your adult children? What kind of support can you offer them in return?
- Beyond finances, what other forms of support are valuable to you and your adult children? How can you show appreciation for non-monetary contributions?

- Do you feel valued and appreciated by your children? Do you have meaningful connections with loved ones and a sense of purpose in life?
- How do you intend to celebrate small wins?
- Create a personalized financial plan with projected future needs.
- Create a list of non-financial ways you and your children can support each other, such as practical help, companionship, and social connections.
- Reflect on your personal values, goals, and sources of joy. Discuss these with your children and explore ways to support each other's well-being.

The relationship between parents and adult children is an ever-changing journey. As we navigate the different chapters of life, it's important to embrace clear communication about financial needs and emotional support. By doing so, we can shine a light the murky crystal ball that often obscures our path, allowing a radiant light to guide us and brighten not only our own lives but also the lives of our adult children and their children. In this, we find solace and unconditional love that make us feel truly at home. So, let's walk this journey and say with confidence, "I am home!"

Conclusion

In this journey, we have illuminated the murky crystal ball that often obscures the path of parenting adult children. A radiant light has been allowed to shine through the crystal ball to guide you and brighten your life. We have navigated through the complexities of the transformative phase of parenting adult children, armed with insights and strategies to build stronger, more communicative relationships. Now, as we conclude our exploration, let's take a moment to reflect on the route that will pave the way for a fulfilling journey of peacefully parenting adult children.

The transition from parenting to guiding, from being the primary decision-maker to allowing our adult children to chart their course, can be exhilarating and grief-inducing. Acknowledge the sense of loss, the echoes of laughter no longer filling our hallways. But beyond the loss, a new chapter unfolds. It is a chance for us to rediscover ourselves, embrace lifelong learning, and strengthen our bonds with our adult children. The empty nest is not an ending but just a start—a time for self-discovery, personal growth, and deeper connection.

Communication is at the heart of this journey—the invisible thread that binds our evolving relationship with our adult children. It is about creating a safe space for vulnerability, authentic conversations, and the freedom to be ourselves. Delve into active listening, immersing ourselves in our adult children's perspectives, and bridging the communication gaps that can lead to misunderstandings and tension. By mastering the transformative power of communication, we can truly see, appreciate, and connect with our loved ones on this ever-evolving journey.

Navigating shifting dynamics requires us to adapt and embrace new roles and responsibilities—navigate the generational divide, bridging the gaps between our experiences and perspectives. Our role as guides, coaches, mentors, and supporters needs to evolve in tandem as our adult children journey through career paths, relationships, and parenthood. We yearn to find the delicate balance of guiding while respecting their autonomy, establishing healthy boundaries, and honoring their individuality. It is through mutual learning, open communication, and shared experiences that we strengthen the bond between generations, creating a relationship of trust, respect, and love.

The financial aspect of parenting adult children is a significant challenge. We learn to shift our perspective and strike a balance between supporting our adult children's financial journey and guiding them toward self-reliance.

As we continue our journey, we remember that life rarely follows a predictable script. Challenges like divorce, addictions, disabilities, and financial struggles may arise, presenting additional complexities to navigate with our adult children. However, we can support them through these special circumstances, strengthening our bond along the way by showing empathy, patience, and a commitment to empowering our adult children while nurturing their well-being.

Building strong and resilient relationships with our adult children requires effort, commitment, and a willingness to adapt. We choose daily to nurture deeper roots and stronger branches within "The Bonding Garden" of our connections, embracing flexibility, understanding, and open lines of communication. By respecting our adult children's individuality, listening with an open mind, and embracing the changes in the family dynamic with joy, we create a solid foundation for a stronger, more resilient bond.

As our adult children become parents themselves, we enter the exciting yet sometimes tricky role of being grandparents. Finding the balance between support and respect for their parenting style is crucial, as is understanding boundaries and offering wisdom without imposing demands. We transition from being solely our adult child's parent to being part of a larger family dynamic, maintaining open communication and an appreciation for the beautiful journey they embark upon.

Yet, we acknowledge that the delicate fabric of parent adult-child relationships can experience hardships, including the painful experience of estrangement. Rebuilding trust and reconnecting demands unwavering patience, consistent actions, and a deep understanding of the complex interplay of vulnerability and fractured trust. Likewise, as life takes unexpected turns, we may find ourselves in a role reversal where our adult children become our support system. Navigating this humbling challenge requires resilience, open-heartedness, and a recognition of the deeper dimensions of emotional support.

This book has changed me in ways I did not expect. It has taught me that I don't need to be perfect as a parent. I have taken my experiences and put them proudly on display. This isn't to insinuate that I have perfected parenting but that I am using my experiences to grow. The research and time I have taken to compile this book have stretched me and shown me that being a human means you will be a lifelong learner. I hope that the insights in this book will push you to read more about peaceful parenting and that you will build stronger and more fulfilling relationships with your adult children. Writing the strategies doesn't mean that I have practiced all of them. In the same way, just reading won't automatically mean you know how to apply the strategies. I have put together practical ways to try and improve your relationship with your adult children. I hope that this book will encourage you to go out there and empower yourself. Let this be the book that inspires you to read up on information, seek help, and pursue the best relationship possible with your adult children.

Having access to all this information is futile if you don't put it into practice. You may feel overwhelmed with the information and strategies, but you can start small and gradually expand. Your circumstances will determine how much and at what pace you will apply them. Be patient with yourself. There is no rush; parenting is a lifelong journey that will evolve over time. Keep the fundamentals of your relationship constant. If the foundation of your relationship with your adult children is strong, it can withstand any changes.

Parenting is a deeply rewarding and enriching experience. It is not always easy, and you may stumble along the way, but with an open mind, an open heart, and a commitment to the fundamental values of love, respect, and support, you can embrace the challenges and rewards that come with parenting adult children. May this book serve as your roadmap, empowering you to embark on this lifelong journey with confidence and resilience. Your future awaits!

Glossary

Bank of Mom and Dad: Parents financially support their adult children.

Boomerang children: Adult children who move back in with their parents after living independently.

Empty nest syndrome: Feelings of sadness or loss experienced by parents when their children leave home.

Extended ease: Grandparenthood is marked by a unique ease and bond with grandchildren.

Failure to launch: A term used to describe adult children who struggle to transition into independent adulthood.

Generation gap: The perceived differences in values, attitudes, and cultural norms between parents and their adult children.

Grown and flown: The phase of life when parents shift their focus from raising children to pursuing their passions and interests.

Helicopter parenting: Overly involved and controlling parenting style, especially with adult children.

Momsplaining (Dadsplaining): Mothers and fathers offering unsolicited advice or information to their adult children.

Reverse parenting: When adult children take on the role of providing care and supporting their aging parents.

Sandwich generation: Individuals who are simultaneously caring for their children and aging parents.

Second act: The phase of life when parents shift their focus from raising children to pursuing their passions and interests.

Silver splitting: Refers to couples who divorce later in life, often after their adult children have left home.

References

Barroso, A., Parker, K., & Fry, R. (2019, October 23). *Majority of Americans say parents are doing too much for their young adult children.* Pew Research Center. https://www.pewresearch.org/social-trends/2019/10/23/majority-of-americans-say-parents-are-doing-too-much-for-their-young-adult-children/

Birditt, K. S., Miller, L. M., Fingerman, K. L., & Lefkowitz, E. S. (2009). Tensions in the parent and adult child relationship: Links to solidarity and ambivalence. *Psychol Aging, 24*(2), 287–295. https://www.ncbi.nlm.nih.gov/pmc/articles/PMC2690709/

Brotherson, S., Langerud, B., & Saxena, D. (2020, October). *The art of grandparenting no. 1: Becoming a grandparent.* North Dakota State University. https://www.ag.ndsu.edu/publications/kids-family/the-art-of-grandparenting-no-1-in-the-series#section-5

Busco, A. G. (2020, September 15). *What if I don't want the divorce? Can I stop it?* Psychologytoday. https://www.psychologytoday.com/za/blog/better-divorce/202009/what-if-i-dont-want-the-divorce-can-i-stop-it

Caine, N. (n.d.). *Empty nest support services.* Emptynestsupport. https://www.emptynestsupport.com/

Canadian Paediatric Society. (2018, August) *Helping children cope with separation and divorce.* Caring for Kids. https://caringforkids.cps.ca/handouts/mentalhealth/separation_and_divorce

Cherry, K. (2023, November 14). *Generativity vs. stagnation in psychosocial development.* Verywell Mind. https://www.verywellmind.com/generativity-versus-stagnation-2795734

Davis, D. (2017, January 27). *The secrets to communicating with your adult children.* Grand. https://www.grandmagazine.com/2017/01/communicating-adult-children/

Dickler, J. (2022, December 21). *As the cost of living skyrockets, nearly 1 in 3 adults rely on their parents for financial support.* CNBC. https://www.cnbc.com/2022/12/21/amid-inflation-nearly-1-in-3-adults-get-financial-help-from-parents.html

Fuscalos, D. (2022, June 20). *Is a gray divorce inevitable? 5 steps women should take.* AARP. https://www.aarp.org/money/budgeting-saving/info-2022/gray-divorce-asset-protection-for-women.html

Gilligan, M., Suitor, J. J., & Pillemer, K. (2015). Estrangement between mothers and adult children: The role of norms and values. *Journal of Marriage and Family, 77*(4), 908-920. https://doi.org/10.1111/jomf.12207

Huff, C. (2023, November 1) *More couples are divorcing after age 50 than ever before. Psychologists are helping them navigate the big changes.* American Psychological Association. https://www.apa.org/monitor/2023/11/navigating-late-in-life-divorce#:~:text=In%201990%2C%208.7%25%20of%20all,9%2C%202022i

Karney, B. R., & Bradbury, T. N. (2020). Research on marital satisfaction and stability in the 2010s: Challenging conventional wisdom. *Journal of Marriage and Family, 82*(1), 100–116. https://doi.org/10.1111/jomf.12635

Kemp, G., Smith, M. A., & Segal, J. (2023, February 24). *Children and divorce.* HelpGuide. https://www.helpguide.org/articles/parenting-family/children-and-divorce.htm#:~:text=Kids%20may%20feel%20shocked%2C%20uncertain,measure%20of%20grief%20and%20hardship

Life after divorce: How you can start again. (2022, May 8). Cleveland Clinic. https://health.clevelandclinic.org/life-after-divorce

Maijala, E., Uusiautti, S., & Määttä, K. (2012). Grandparental love: A challenge or richness?, *Early Child Development and Care, 183*(5), 627-642. http://dx.doi.org/10.1080/03004430.2012.678491

Mangrum, D., Scally, J., & Wang, C. (2022, August 9). *Three key facts from the Center for Microeconomic Data's 2022 student loan update.* Federal Reserve Bank of New York. *https://libertystreeteconomics.newyorkfed.org/2022/08/three-key-facts-from-the-center-for-microeconomic-datas-2022-student-loan-update/*

Noeder, M. (2023). *Dealing with divorce.* Nemours Teens Health. https://kidshealth.org/en/teens/deal-with-divorce.prt-en.html

PureWow. (2022, January 13). *You're not a kid anymore. So why does your parents' divorce suck so much?* Yahoo! Life. https://www.yahoo.com/lifestyle/not-kid-anymore-why-does-200000567.html?guccounter=1&guce_referrer=aHR0cHM6Ly93d3cuZ29vZ2xlLmNvbS8&guce_referrer_sig=AQAAALcUuvcCW0ZLaUqIktZ4_jPQz7q86hZd8uWn3Cj33d1CB_Ysu8pxpFmfGFpC7jjXLaB9mIf_8C-bBRb1hwCGN4KAmeBXUjTMSkwFjghQpKVQYSfTuQaL974Hg8ECWvtbMq8lBYnEU24R7vi5x5g619F_FPCXSUN_5FbjBzrgGV6p

RBC Wealth Management. (2024, February 7). *Global insight.* https://ca.rbcwealthmanagement.com/documents/10180/0/monthlyx.pdf

Singletary, M. (2023, November 17). *Our kids don't want our paid-off house - or our ashes.* The Washington Post. https://www.washingtonpost.com/business/2023/11/17/kids-sell-parents-inherited-house/

Steinberg, L. (2023, May). *Speaking of psychology: How parents and their adult children can build strong relationships.* American Psychological Association. https://www.apa.org/news/podcasts/speaking-of-psychology/parent-adult-children-relationships

Tyrrell, P., Harberger, S., Schoo, C, & Siddiqui, W. (2023, February 26). *Kubler-Ross stages of dying and subsequent models of grief.* National Library of Medicine. https://www.ncbi.nlm.nih.gov/books/NBK507885/

United States Census Bureau. (2022, November 17). *America's families and living arrangements: 2022.* https://www.census.gov/data/tables/2022/demo/families/cps-2022.html

U.S. Bureau of Labor Statistics. (2019, March 1). *Employment of people with a disability in 2018.* The Economics Daily. https://www.bls.gov/opub/ted/2019/employment-of-people-with-a-disability-in-2018.htm

Made in the USA
Monee, IL
01 September 2024

64985271R10067